Disclaimer

All erudition contained in this book is given for informational and educational purposes only. The author is not in any way accountable for any results or outcomes that emanate from using this material. Constructive attempts have been made to provide information that is both accurate and effective, but the author is not bound for the accuracy or use/misuse of this information.

The Complete Apocrypha Of The Ethiopian Bible

The 88 Missing and Lost Books of the Bible

Sebastian J. Moore and Ethan Foster

Contents

Jubilees

It happened in the first year of the exodus of the children of Israel out of Egypt, in the third month, on the sixteenth day of the month, that God spoke to Moses, saying, "Come up to Me on the Mountain, and I will give you two tablets of stone of the law and the commandment, which I have written, that you may teach them."

Moses went up into the mountain of God, and the glory of the Lord rested on Mount Sinai, and a cloud overshadowed it six days. He called to Moses on the seventh day out of the middle of the cloud, and the appearance of the glory of the Lord was like a flame on the top of the mountain. Moses was on the mountain forty days and forty nights, and God taught him the earlier and the later history of the division of all the days of the law and of the testimony. He said, "Open your heart to every word which I shall speak to you on this mountain, and write them in a book in order that their generations may see how I have not forsaken them for all the evil which they have committed when they transgressed the covenant which I establish between Me and you for their generations this day on Mount Sinai. It will come to pass when all these things come on them, that they will recognize that I am more righteous than they in all their judgments and in all their actions, and they will recognize that I have truly been with them."

When we saw His works, we praised Him, and worshiped Him because of all His works; for seven great works He created on the first day. On the second day He created the sky between the waters (above and below), and the waters were divided on that day. Half of them went up above the sky and half of them went down below the sky that was in the middle over the face of the whole earth. And this was the only work God created on the second day. On the third day He commanded the waters to pass from off the face of the whole earth into one place, and the dry land to appear. The waters did as He commanded them, and they receded from off the face of the earth into one place, and the dry land appeared. On that day He created for them all the seas according to their separate gathering-places, and all the rivers, and the gatherings of the waters in the mountains and on all the earth, and all the lakes, and all the dew of the earth, and the seed which is sown, and all sprouting things, and fruit bearing trees, and trees of the wood, and the garden of Eden, in Eden and throughout. These four great works God created on the third day.

On the sixth day of the second week, according to the word of God, we brought to Adam all the beasts, and all the cattle, and all the birds, and everything that moves on the earth, and everything that moves in the water, according to their kinds, and according to their types, the beasts on the first day; the cattle on the second day; the birds on the third day; and all that moves on the earth on the fourth day;

and all that moves in the water on the fifth day. And Adam named them all by their respective names. As he called them, so was their name. On these five days Adam saw all these, male and female, according to every kind that was on the earth, but he was alone and found no helpmate.

The Lord said to us, "It is not good that the man should be alone, let us make a helpmate for him." And the Lord our God caused a deep sleep to fall on him, and he slept, and He took from Adam a rib from among his ribs for the woman, and this rib was the origin of the woman. And He built up the flesh in its place, and built the woman. He awakened Adam out of his sleep and on awakening he rose on the sixth day, and He brought her to him, and he knew her, and said to her, "This is now bone of my bones and flesh of my flesh; she shall be called my wife; because she was taken from her husband." Therefore shall man and wife become one and therefore shall a man leave his father and his mother, and cling to his wife, and they shall be one flesh. In the first week Adam was created, and from his rib, his wife. In the second week God showed her to him, and for this reason the commandment was given to keep in their defilement. A male should be purified in seven days, and for a female twice seven days. After Adam had completed forty days in the land where he had been created, we brought him into the garden of Eden to till and keep it, but his wife we brought in on the eightieth day, and after this she entered into the garden of Eden.

When the children of men began to multiply on the face of the earth and daughters were born to them, and the angels of God saw them on a certain year of this jubilee, that they were beautiful, and they took themselves wives of all whom they chose, and they gave birth to their sons and they were giants. Because of them lawlessness increased on the earth and all flesh corrupted its way. Men and cattle and beasts and birds and everything that walked on the earth were all corrupted in their ways and their orders, and they began to devour each other. Lawlessness increased on the earth and the imagination and thoughts of all men were continually, totally evil. God looked on the earth, and saw it was corrupt, and all flesh had corrupted its orders, and all that were on the earth had committed all manner of evil before His eyes. He said that He would destroy man and all flesh on the face of the earth that He had created. But Noah found grace before the eyes of the Lord.

And against the angels whom He had sent on the earth, He had boiling anger, and He gave commandment to root them out of all their dominion, and He commanded us to bind them in the depths of the earth, and look, they are bound in the middle of the earth, and are kept separate. And against their sons went out a command from His mouth that they should be killed with the sword, and be left under heaven.

And the Lord smelled the good and pleasing odor, and He made a covenant with Noah that there should not be any more floods to destroy the earth; that all the days of the earth seed-time and harvest should never cease; cold and heat, and summer and winter, and day and night should not change their order, nor cease forever. "Increase and multiply on the earth, and become many, and be a blessing on it. I will inspire the fear of you and the dread of you in everything that is on earth and in the sea. Look, I have given you all beasts, and all winged things, and everything that moves on the earth, and the fish in the waters, and all things for food; as the green herbs, I have given you all things to eat. But you shall not eat anything live or with blood in it, for the life of all flesh is in the blood, or your blood of your lives will be required. At the hand of every man, at the hand of every beast will I require the blood of man. Whoever sheds man's blood by man shall his blood be shed, for in the image of God He made man. Increase, and multiply on the earth."

Noah and his sons swore that they would not eat any blood that was in any flesh, and he made a covenant before the Lord God forever throughout all the generations of the earth in this month. Because of this He spoke to you that you should make a covenant with the children of Israel with an oath. In this month, on the mountain you should sprinkle blood on them because of all the words of the covenant, which the Lord made with them forever. This testimony is written concerning you that you should observe it continually, so that you should not eat on any day any blood of beasts or birds or cattle during all the days of the earth, and the man who eats the blood of beast or of cattle or of birds during all the days of the earth, he and his offspring shall be rooted out of the land. And you will command the children of Israel to eat no blood, so that their names and their offspring may be before the Lord our God continually. There is no limit of days, for this law. It is forever. They shall observe it throughout their generations, so that they may continue supplicating on your behalf with blood before the altar; every day and at the time of morning and evening they shall seek forgiveness on your behalf perpetually before the Lord that they may keep it and not be rooted out.

In the thirtieth jubilee, in the second week, in the first year of it, he took to himself a wife, and her name was Melka, the daughter of Madai, the son of Japheth, and in the fourth year he begat a son, and called his name Shelah; for he said, "Truly I have been sent." Shelah grew up and took to himself a wife, and her name was Mu' ak, the daughter of Kesed, his father's brother, in the one and thirtieth jubilee, in the fifth week, in the first year of it. And she gave birth to a son in the fifth year of it, and he called his name Eber, and he took to himself a wife, and her name was Azurad, the daughter of Nebrod, in the thirty-second jubilee, in the seventh week, in the third year of it.

In the sixth year of it, she gave birth to a son, and he called his name Peleg, for in the days when he was born the children of Noah began to divide the earth among themselves, for this reason he called his name Peleg. They divided it secretly among themselves, and told it to Noah.

In the beginning of the thirty-third jubilee they divided the earth into three parts, for Shem and Ham and Japheth, according to the inheritance of each, in the first year in the first week, when one of us (angels) who had been sent, was with them. He called his sons, and they drew close to him, they and their children, and he divided the earth into the lots, which his three sons were to take in possession, and they reached out their hands, and took the writing out of the arms of Noah, their father. There came out on the writing as Shem's lot the middle of the earth that he should take as an inheritance for himself and for his sons for the generations of eternity. From the middle of the mountain range of Rafa, from the mouth of the water from the river Tina, and his portion goes towards the west through the middle of this river, and it extends until it reaches the water of the abysses, out of which this river goes out and pours its waters into the sea Me' at, and this river flows into the great sea. All that is towards the north is Japheth's, and all that is towards the south belongs to Shem. And it extends until it reaches Karaso, this is in the center of the tongue of land that looks towards the south.

Ham divided among his sons, and the first portion came out for Cush towards the east, and to the west of him for Mizraim, and to the west of him for Put, and to the west of him on the sea for Canaan. Shem also divided among his sons, and the first portion came out for Ham and his sons, to the east of the river Tigris until it approaches the east, the whole land of India, and on the Red Sea on its coast, and the waters of Dedan, and all the mountains of Mebri and Ela, and all the land of Susan and all that is on the side of Pharnak to the Red Sea and the river Tina.

Asshur received the second Portion, all the land of Asshur and Nineveh and Shinar and to the border of India, and it ascends and skirts the river. Arpachshad received the third portion, all the land of the region of the Chaldees to the east of the Euphrates, bordering on the Red Sea, and all the waters of the desert close to the tongue of the sea which looks towards Egypt, all the land of Lebanon and Sanir and Amana to the border of the Euphrates. Aram received the fourth portion, all the land of Mesopotamia between the Tigris and the Euphrates to the north of the Chaldees to the border of the mountains of Asshur and the land of Arara. Lud got the fifth portion, the mountains of Asshur and all surrounding to them until it reaches the Great Sea, and until it reaches the east of Asshur his brother.

In the thirty-fifth jubilee, in the third week, in the first year of it, Reu took to himself a wife, and her name was Ora, the daughter of Ur, the son of Kesed, and she gave birth to a son, and he called his name Seroh, in the seventh year of this week in this jubilee. The sons of Noah began to war with each other, to take captives and kill each other, and to shed the blood of men on the earth, and to eat blood, and to build strong cities, and walls, and towers, and individuals began to exalt themselves above the nation, and to establish kingdoms, and to go to war, people against people, and nation against nation, and city against city, and all began to do evil, and to acquire arms, and to teach their sons war, and they began to capture cities, and to sell male and female slaves. Ur, the son of Kesed, built the city of Ara of the Chaldees, and called its name after his own name and the name of his father. And they made themselves molten images, and they worshipped the idols and the molten image they had made for themselves, and they began to make graven images and unclean and shadowy presence, and malevolent and malicious spirits assisted and seduced them into committing transgression and uncleanness. Prince Mastema exerted himself to do all this, and he sent out other spirits, which were put under his control, to do all manner of wrong and sin, and all manner of transgression, to corrupt and destroy, and to shed blood on the earth. For this reason he called the name of Seroh, Serug, for every one turned to do all manner of sin and transgression.

In the fifth year of the fourth week of this jubilee, in the third month, in the middle of the month, Abram celebrated the feast of the first-fruits of the grain harvest. And he made new offerings on the altar, the first-fruits of the produce to the Lord, a heifer, and a goat, and a sheep on the altar as a burnt sacrifice to the Lord; their fruit offerings and their drink offerings he offered on the altar with frankincense.

The Lord appeared to Abram, and said to him, "I am God Almighty. Examine yourself and demonstrate yourself before me and be perfect. I will make My covenant between Me and you, and I will multiply you greatly." Abram fell on his face, and God talked with him, and said, "My law is with you, and you will be the father of many nations. Neither shall your name any more be called Abram, but your name from now on, even forever, shall be Abraham.

For I have made you the father of many nations. I will make you very great, and I will make you into nations, and kings shall come forth from you. I shall establish My covenant between Me and you, and your offspring after you, throughout their generations, for an eternal covenant, so that I may be a God to you, and to your offspring after you. You may possess the land where you have been a sojourner, the land of Canaan, and you will possess it forever, and I will be their God."

The Lord said to Abraham, "Keep my covenant, you and your offspring after you, and circumcise every male among you, and circumcise your foreskins, and it shall be a token of an eternal covenant between Me and you." In the first year of the first week in the forty-second jubilee, Abraham returned and lived across from Hebron, in Kirjath Arba for two weeks of years. In the first year of the third week of this jubilee the days of the life of Sarah were completed, and she died in Hebron. Abraham went to mourn over her and bury her, and we tested him to see if his spirit was patient and he had neither anger nor contempt in the words of his mouth, and he was found patient in this and was not disturbed. In patience of spirit he discussed with the children of Heth that they should give him a place in which to bury his dead. And the Lord gave him grace before all who saw him, and he asked the sons of Heth in gentleness, and they gave him the land of the double cave over beside Mamre, that is Hebron, for four hundred pieces of silver.

They said to him, "We shall give it to you for nothing," but he would not take it from them for nothing, for he gave the price of the place and paid the money in full. And he bowed down before them twice, and after this he buried his dead in the double cave. All the days of the life of Sarah were one hundred and twenty-seven years, that is, two jubilees and four weeks and one year, these are the days of the years of the life of Sarah.

1 Enoch

The words of the blessing of Enoch, with which he blessed the elect and righteous, who will be living in the day of tribulation, when all the wicked and godless are to be removed. And he began his story saying: Enoch a righteous man, whose eyes were opened by God, saw the vision of the Holy One in heaven, which the angels showed me, and I heard everything from them, and I saw and understood, but it was not for this generation, but for a remote one which is to come. Concerning the elect I said, as I began my story concerning them: The Holy Great One will come out from His dwelling, And the eternal God will tread on the earth, (even) on Mount Sinai, and appear in the strength of His might from heaven.

And the light of God shall shine on them. And behold! He comes with ten thousand of His holy ones (saints) to execute judgment on all, and to destroy all the ungodly (wicked); and to convict all flesh of all the works of their ungodliness which they have ungodly committed, and of all the hard things which ungodly sinners have spoken against Him. And all of them together went and took wives for themselves, each choosing one for himself, and they began to go in to them and to defile themselves with sex with them, And the angels taught them charms and spells, and the cutting of roots, and made them acquainted with plants. And the women became pregnant, and they bare large giants, whose height was three thousand cubits (ells).

The giants consumed all the work and toil of men. And when men could no longer sustain them, the giants turned against them and devoured mankind. And they began to sin against birds, and beasts, and reptiles, and fish, and to devour one another's flesh, and drank the blood. Then the earth laid accusation against the lawless ones. And Enoch went and said: "I Azazel, you shall have no peace: a severe sentence has been passed against you that you should be bound: And you shall not have rest or mercy (toleration nor request granted), because of the unrighteousness which you have taught, and because of all the works of godlessness, And unrighteousness and sin which you have shown to men."

Then I went and spoke to them all together, and they were all afraid, and fear and trembling seized them. And they asked me to write a petition for them that they might find forgiveness, and to read their petition in the presence of the Lord of heaven. They had been forbidden to speak (with Him) nor were they to lift up their eyes to heaven for shame of their sins because they had been condemned. Then I wrote out their petition, and the prayer in regard to their spirits and their deeds individually and in regard to their requests that they should obtain forgiveness and forbearance.

And I went off and sat down at the waters of Dan, in the land of Dan, to the southwest of Hermon: I read their petition until I fell asleep.

And I had a dream, and I saw a vision of their chastisement, and a voice came to me that I would reprimand (reprove) them. And when I awoke, I came to them, and they were all sitting gathered together, weeping in Abelsjail, which is between Lebanon and Seneser, with their faces covered. And He answered and said to me, and I heard His voice: 'Do not be afraid, Enoch, you righteous man and scribe of righteousness. Approach and hear my voice. Go and say to the Watchers of heaven, for whom you have come to intercede: "You should intercede for men, and not men for you." Why and for what cause have you left the high, holy, and eternal heaven, and had sex with women, and defiled yourselves with the daughters of men and taken to yourselves wives, and done like the children of earth, and begotten giants (as your) sons?

Though you were holy, spiritual, living the eternal life, you have defiled yourselves with the blood of women, and have begotten children with the blood of flesh, and, as the children of men, you have lusted after flesh and blood like those who die and are killed. This is why I have given men wives, that they might impregnate them, and have children by them, that deeds might continue on the earth. But you were formerly spiritual, living the eternal life, and immortal for all generations of the world. Therefore I have not appointed wives for you; you are spiritual beings of heaven, and in heaven was your dwelling place.

And at the death of the giants, spirits will go out and shall destroy without incurring judgment, coming from their bodies their flesh shall be destroy until the day of the consummation, the great judgment in which the age shall be consummated, over the Watchers and the godless, and shall be wholly consummated.' And now as to the Watchers who have sent you to intercede for them, who had been in heaven before, (Say to them): "You were in heaven, but all the mysteries of heaven had not been revealed to you, and you knew worthless ones, and these in the hardness of your hearts you have made known to the women, and through these mysteries women and men work much evil on earth." Say to them therefore: " You have no peace." I saw the storehouse of all the winds: I saw how He had adorned the whole creation with them and the firm foundations of the earth.

And I saw the corner-stone of the earth: I saw the four winds which support the earth and the firmament of the heaven. I saw how the winds stretch out the height of heaven, and have their station between heaven and earth; these are the pillars of heaven. I saw the winds of heaven which turn and bring the sky and the sun and all the stars to their setting place.

I saw the winds on the earth carrying the clouds: I saw the paths of the angels. I saw at the end of the earth the firmament of heaven above. And I continued south and saw a place which burns day and night, where there are seven mountains of magnificent stones, three towards the east, and three towards the south. And as for those towards the east, they were of colored stone, and one of pearl, and one of jacinth (a stone of healing), and those towards the south of red stone. But the middle one reached to heaven like the throne of God, and was made of alabaster. And the summit of the throne was of sapphire.

And I saw a great abyss of the earth, with pillars of heavenly fire, and I saw among them fiery pillars of Heaven, which were falling, And as regards both height and depth, they were immeasurable. And beyond that abyss I saw a place which had no firmament of heaven above, and no firmly founded earth beneath it: there was no water on it, and no birds, But it was a desert and a horrible place. I saw seven stars like great burning mountains, And an angel questioned me regarding them. The angel said: 'This place is the end of heaven and earth.'

2 Enoch (Slavonic)

And there appeared to me two men, exceeding big, so that I never saw such on earth; their faces were shining like the sun, their eyes too were like a burning light, and from their lips was fire coming forth with clothing and singing of various kinds in appearance purple, their wings were brighter than gold, their hands whiter than snow. They were standing at the head of my couch and began to call me by my name. And I arose from my sleep and saw clearly those two men standing in front of me.

And I saluted them and was seized with fear and the appearance of my face was changed from terror, and those men said to me: 'Have courage, Enoch, do not fear; the eternal God sent us to thee, and lo! thou shalt to-day ascend with us into heaven, and thou shalt tell thy sons and all thy household all that they shall do without thee on earth in thy house, and let no one seek thee till the Lord return thee to them.' And I made haste to obey them and went out from my house, and made to the doors, as it was ordered me, and summoned my sons Mathusal and Regim and Gaidad and made known to them all the marvels those men had told me.

It came to pass, when Enoch had told his sons, that the angels took him on to their wings and bore him up on to the first heaven and placed him on the clouds. And there I looked, and again I looked higher, and saw the ether, and they placed me on the first heaven and showed me a very great Sea, greater than the earthly sea. Of the Angels ruling the stars. They brought before my face the elders and rulers of the stellar orders, and showed me two hundred angels, who rule the stars and their services to the heavens, and fly with their wings and come round all those who sail.

They showed me the treasure-house of the dew, like oil of the olive, and the appearance of its form, as of all the flowers of the earth; further many angels guarding the treasure-houses of these things, and how they are made to shut and open. And those men took me and led me up on to the second heaven, and showed me darkness, greater than earthly darkness, and there I saw prisoners hanging, watched, awaiting the great and boundless judgment, and these angels were dark-looking, more than earthly darkness, and incessantly making weeping through all hours. And I said to the men who were with me: 'Wherefore are these incessantly tortured?' they answered me: 'These are God's apostates, who obeyed not God's commands, but took counsel with their own will, and turned away with their prince, who also is fastened on the fifth heaven.'

And I felt great pity for them, and they saluted me, and said to me:

'Man of God, pray for us to the Lord'; and I answered to them: 'Who am I, a mortal man, that I should pray for angels? Who knoweth whither I go, or what will befall me? Or who will pray for me?' And those men took me thence, and led me up on to the third heaven, and placed me there; and I looked downwards, and saw the produce of these places, such as has never been known for goodness. And I saw all the sweet-flowering trees and beheld their fruits, which were sweet-smelling, and all the foods borne by them bubbling with fragrant exhalation. And in the midst of the trees that of life, in that place whereon the Lord rests, when he goes up into paradise; and this tree is of ineffable goodness and fragrance, and adorned more than every existing thing; and on all sides it is in form gold-looking and vermilion and fire-like and covers all, and it has produce from all fruits. Its root is in the garden at the earth's end.

And paradise is between corruptibility and incorruptibility. And those two men led me upon to the Northern side, and showed me there a very terrible place, and there were all manner of tortures in that place: cruel darkness and unilluminated gloom, and there is no light there, but murky fire constantly flameth aloft, and that whole place is everywhere fire, and everywhere there is frost and ice, thirst and shivering, while the bonds are very cruel, and the angels fearful and merciless, bearing angry weapons, merciless torture, and I said: 'Woe, woe, how very terrible is this place.'

And those men said to me: This place, O Enoch, is prepared for those who dishonour God, who on earth practise sin against nature, which is child-corruption after the sodomitic fashion, magic-making, enchantments and devilish witchcrafts, and who boast of their wicked deeds, stealing, lies, calumnies, envy, rancour, fornication, murder, and who, accursed, steal the souls of men, who, seeing the poor take away their goods and themselves wax rich, injuring them for other men's goods; who being able to satisfy the empty, made the hungering to die; being able to clothe, stripped the naked; and who knew not their creator, and bowed down to soulless gods, who cannot see nor hear, vain gods, who also built hewn images and bow down to unclean handiwork, for all these is prepared this place amongst these, for eternal inheritance.

Those men took me, and led me up on to the fourth heaven, and showed me all the successive goings, and all the rays of the light of sun and moon. And I measured their goings and compared their light, and saw that the sun's light is greater than the moon's. Its circle and the wheels on which it goes always, like a wind going past with very marvellous speed, and day and night it has no rest.

Its passage and return are accompanied by four great stars, and each star has under it a thousand stars, to the right of the sun's wheel, and by four to the left, each having under it a thousand stars, altogether eight thousand, issuing with the sun continually. And by day fifteen myriads of angels attend it, and by night a thousand.

And I looked and saw other flying elements of the sun, whose names are Phoenixes and Chalkydri, marvellous and wonderful, with feet and tails in the form of a lion, and a crocodile's head, their appearance is empurpled, like the rainbow; their size is nine hundred measures, their wings are like those of angels, each has twelve, and they attend and accompany the sun, bearing heat and dew, as it is ordered them from God. Thus the sun revolves and goes, and rises under the heaven, and its course goes under the earth with the light of its rays incessantly.

The angels took Enoch and placed him in the east at the sun's gates.

3 Enoch (Hebrew)

When R. Ishmael ascended to heaven to behold the vision of the Merkaba, he entered the six Halls, one within the other. Upon reaching the door of the seventh Hall, he stood still in prayer before the Holy One, lifting up his eyes towards the Divine Majesty. He prayed, invoking the merit of Aaron, the son of Amram, asking for protection from Qafsiel, the prince, and the angels with him. In response, the Holy One sent Metatron, His Servant, the angel, the Prince of the Presence, to save Ishmael from their grasp. Metatron spread his wings and joyfully came to meet Ishmael, taking him by the hand in the sight of all, leading him to behold the picture of the Merkaba.

Entering the seventh Hall, Ishmael was placed before the Holy One to behold the Merkaba. The princes of the Merkaba and the flaming Seraphim fixed their eyes upon him, causing him to tremble and shudder. However, upon the rebuke of the Holy One, they covered their eyes before Ishmael, preventing further fear. Metatron then restored Ishmael's spirit and put him upon his feet. Yet, Ishmael found himself lacking strength to offer a song before the Throne of Glory until an hour had passed.

After one hour, the Holy One opened the gates of Shekina to Ishmael, enlightening his eyes and heart with words of psalm, song, praise, and thanksgiving. As Ishmael opened his mouth to sing before the Holy One, the Holy Chayyoth beneath and above the Throne of Glory joined in, chanting the Qedushsha.

From the time of the expulsion of the first Adam from the Garden of Eden, Shekina dwelled upon a Kerub under the Tree of Life. The ministering angels gathered and descended from heaven to do the will of the Holy One in the world. The first man and his generation sat outside the gate of the Garden, beholding the radiant appearance of the Shekina. The splendor of the Shekina traversed the world with a brilliance surpassing that of the sun, offering protection and blessing to those who embraced it.

However, during the generation of Enosh, the head of all idol worshippers, humanity turned to idolatry. Enosh's generation erected idols throughout the world, bringing down celestial bodies to attend them. The ministering angels brought charges against humanity before the Holy One, questioning His presence among idol worshippers. In response, the Holy One lifted His Shekina from the earth, departing from their midst.

At that moment, the ministering angels, along with the troops of hosts and the armies of Araboth, surrounded the Shekina with songs and trumpets as it ascended to the high heavens.

Baruch

These are the words of the book which Baruch the son of Neraiah, son of Mahseiah, son of Zedekiah, son of Hasadiah, son of Hilkiah, wrote in Babylon, in the fifth year, on the seventh day of the month, at the time when the Chaldeans took Jerusalem and burned it with fire. Baruch read the words of this book in the hearing of Jeconiah the son of Jehoiakim, king of Judah, and in the hearing of all the people who came to hear the book, and in the hearing of the mighty men and the princes, and in the hearing of the elders, and in the hearing of all the people, small and great, all who dwelt in Babylon by the river Sud.

Then they wept, and fasted, and prayed before the Lord; and they collected money, each giving what he could; and they sent it to Jerusalem to Jehoiakim the high priest, the son of Hilkiah, son of Shallum, and to the priests, and to all the people who were present with him in Jerusalem. At the same time, on the tenth day of Sivan, Baruch took the vessels of the house of the Lord, which had been carried away from the temple, to return them to the land of Judah -- the silver vessels which Zedekiah the son of Josiah, king of Judah, had made, after Nebuchadnezzar king of Babylon had carried away from Jerusalem Jeconiah and the princes and the prisoners and the mighty men and the people of the land, and brought them to Babylon.

And they said: "Herewith we send you money; so buy with the money burnt offerings and sin offerings and incense, and prepare a cereal offering, and offer them upon the altar of the Lord our God; and pray for the life of Nebuchadnezzar king of Babylon, and for the life of Belshazzar his son, that their days on earth may be like the days of heaven. And the Lord will give us strength, and he will give light to our eyes, and we shall live under the protection of Nebuchadnezzar king of Babylon, and under the protection of Belshazzar his son, and we shall serve them many days and find favor in their sight. And pray for us to the Lord our God, for we have sinned against the Lord our God, and to this day the anger of the Lord and his wrath have not turned away from us.

And you shall read this book which we are sending you, to make your confession in the house of the Lord on the days of the feasts and at appointed seasons. And you shall say: Righteousness belongs to the Lord our God, but confusion of face, as at this day, to us, to the men of Judah, to the inhabitants of Jerusalem, and to our kings and our princes and our priests and our prophets and our fathers, because we have sinned before the Lord, and have disobeyed him, and have not heeded the voice of the Lord our God, to walk in the statutes of the Lord which he set before us.

From the day when the Lord brought our fathers out of the land of Egypt until today, we have been disobedient to the Lord our God, and we have been negligent, in not heeding his voice. So to this day there have clung to us the calamities and the curse which the Lord declared through Moses his servant at the time when he brought our fathers out of the land of Egypt to give to us a land flowing with milk and honey. We did not heed the voice of the Lord our God in all the words of the prophets whom he sent to us, but we each followed the intent of his own wicked heart by serving other gods and doing what is evil in the sight of the Lord our God.

Take off the garment of your sorrow and affliction, O Jerusalem, and put on for ever the beauty of the glory from God. Put on the robe of the righteousness from God; put on your head the diadem of the glory of the Everlasting. For God will show your splendor everywhere under heaven. For your name will for ever be called by God, 'Peace of righteousness and glory of godliness.'

Arise, O Jerusalem, stand upon the height and look toward the east, and see your children gathered from west and east, at the word of the Holy One, rejoicing that God has remembered them. For they went forth from you on foot, led away by their enemies; but God will bring them back to you, carried in glory, as on a royal throne. For God has ordered that every high mountain and the everlasting hills be made low and the valleys filled up, to make level ground, so that Israel may walk safely in the glory of God."

The woods and every fragrant tree have shaded Israel at God's command. For God will lead Israel with joy, in the light of his glory, with the mercy and righteousness that come from him.

Jasher

And God said, "Let us make man in our image, after our likeness," and God created man in his own image. And God formed man from the ground, and he blew into his nostrils the breath of life, and man became a living soul endowed with speech. And the Lord said, "It is not good for man to be alone; I will make unto him a helpmeet." And the Lord caused a deep sleep to fall upon Adam, and he slept, and he took away one of his ribs, and he built flesh upon it, and formed it and brought it to Adam, and Adam awoke from his sleep, and behold a woman was standing before him. And he said, "This is a bone of my bones and it shall be called woman, for this has been taken from man"; and Adam called her name Eve, for she was the mother of all living.

And God blessed them and called their names Adam and Eve in the day that he created them, and the Lord God said, "Be fruitful and multiply and fill the earth." And the Lord God took Adam and his wife, and he placed them in the garden of Eden to dress it and to keep it; and he commanded them and said unto them, "From every tree of the garden you may eat, but from the tree of the knowledge of good and evil you shall not eat, for in the day that you eat thereof you shall surely die." And when God had blessed and commanded them, he went from them, and Adam and his wife dwelt in the garden according to the command which the Lord had commanded them.

And the serpent, which God had created with them in the earth, came to them to incite them to transgress the command of God which he had commanded them. And the serpent enticed and persuaded the woman to eat from the tree of knowledge, and the woman hearkened to the voice of the serpent, and she transgressed the word of God, and took from the tree of the knowledge of good and evil, and she ate, and she took from it and gave also to her husband and he ate. And Adam and his wife transgressed the command of God which he commanded them, and God knew it, and his anger was kindled against them and he cursed them. And the Lord God drove them that day from the garden of Eden, to till the ground from which they were taken, and they went and dwelt at the east of the garden of Eden; and Adam knew his wife Eve and she bore two sons and three daughters.

And it was in the hundred and thirtieth year of the life of Adam upon the earth, that he again knew Eve his wife, and she conceived and bare a son in his likeness and in his image, and she called his name Seth, saying, "Because God has appointed me another seed in the place of Abel, for Cain has slain him."

And Seth lived one hundred and five years, and he begat a son; and Seth called the name of his son Enosh, saying, "Because in that time the sons of men began to multiply, and to afflict their souls and hearts by transgressing and rebelling against God."

And it was in the days of Enosh that the sons of men continued to rebel and transgress against God, to increase the anger of the Lord against the sons of men. And the sons of men went and they served other gods, and they forgot the Lord who had created them in the earth: and in those days the sons of men made images of brass and iron, wood and stone, and they bowed down and served them.

And every man made his god and they bowed down to them, and the sons of men forsook the Lord all the days of Enosh and his children; and the anger of the Lord was kindled on account of their works and abominations which they did in the earth. And the Lord caused the waters of the river Gihon to overwhelm them, and he destroyed and consumed them, and he destroyed the third part of the earth, and notwithstanding this, the sons of men did not turn from their evil ways, and their hands were yet extended to do evil in the sight of the Lord.

And all the days that Enoch lived upon earth, were three hundred and sixty-five years. And when Enoch had ascended into heaven, all the kings of the earth rose and took Methuselah his son and anointed him, and they caused him to reign over them in the place of his father. And Methuselah acted uprightly in the sight of God, as his father Enoch had taught him, and he likewise during the whole of his life taught the sons of men wisdom, knowledge and the fear of God, and he did not turn from the good way either to the right or to the left. But in the latter days of Methuselah, the sons of men turned from the Lord, they corrupted the earth, they robbed and plundered each other, and they rebelled against God and they transgressed, and they corrupted their ways, and would not hearken to the voice of Methuselah, but rebelled against him. And the Lord was exceedingly wroth against them, and the Lord continued to destroy the seed in those days, so that there was neither sowing nor reaping in the earth. For when they sowed the ground in order that they might obtain food for their support, behold, thorns and thistles were produced which they did not sow.

And these are the names of the sons of Noah: Japheth, Ham and Shem; and children were born to them after the flood, for they had taken wives before the flood. These are the sons of Japheth; Gomer, Magog, Madai, Javan, Tubal, Meshech, and Tiras, seven sons. And the sons of Gomer were Askinaz, Rephath and Tegarmah. And the sons of

Magog were Elichanaf and Lubal. And the children of Madai were Achon, Zeelo, Chazoni and Lot. And the sons of Javan were Elisha, Tarshish, Chittim and Dudonim.

And the sons of Tubal were Ariphi, Kesed and Taari. And the sons of Meshech were Dedon, Zaron and Shebashni. And the sons of Tiras were Benib, Gera, Lupirion and Gilak; these are the sons of Japheth according to their families, and their numbers in those days were about four hundred and sixty men. And these are the sons of Ham; Cush, Mitzraim, Phut and Canaan, four sons; and the sons of Cush were Seba, Havilah, Sabta, Raama and Satecha, and the sons of Raama were Sheba and Dedan. And the sons of Mitzraim were Lud, Anom and Pathros, Chasloth and Chaphtor. And the sons of Phut were Gebul, Hadan, Benah and Adan.

4 Ezra

Josiah kept the Passover to his Lord in Jerusalem; he killed the Passover lamb on the fourteenth day of the first month, having placed the priests according to their divisions, arrayed in their garments, in the temple of the Lord. And he told the Levites, the temple servants of Israel, that they should sanctify themselves to the Lord and put the holy ark of the Lord in the house which Solomon the king, the son of David, had built; and he said, "You need no longer carry it upon your shoulders.

Now worship the Lord your God and serve his people Israel; and prepare yourselves by your families and kindred, in accordance with the directions of David king of Israel and the magnificence of Solomon his son. Stand in order in the temple according to the groupings of the fathers' houses of you Levites, who minister before your brethren the people of Israel, and kill the Passover lamb and prepare the sacrifices for your brethren, and keep the Passover according to the commandment of the Lord which was given to Moses." And Josiah gave to the people who were present thirty thousand lambs and kids, and three thousand calves; these were given from the king's possessions, as he promised, to the people and the priests and Levites.

And Hilkiah, Zechariah, and Jehiel, the chief officers of the temple, gave to the priests for the Passover two thousand six hundred sheep and three hundred calves. And Jeconiah and Shemaiah and Nethanel his brother, and Hashabiah and Ochiel and Joram, captains over thousands, gave the Levites for the Passover five thousand sheep and seven hundred calves. And this is what took place. The priests and the Levites, properly arrayed and having the unleavened bread, stood according to kindred and the grouping of the fathers' houses, before the people, to make the offering to the Lord as it is written in the book of Moses; this they did in the morning.

They roasted the Passover lamb with fire, as required; and they boiled the sacrifices in brass pots and caldrons, with a pleasing odor, and carried them to all the people. Afterward they prepared the Passover for themselves and for their brethren the priests, the sons of Aaron, because the priests were offering the fat until night; so the Levites prepared it for themselves and for their brethren the priests, the sons of Aaron. And the temple singers, the sons of Asaph, were in their place according to the arrangement made by David, and also Asaph, Zechariah, and Eddinus, who represented the king.

The gatekeepers were at each gate; no one needed to depart from his duties, for their brethren the Levites prepared the Passover for them. So the things that had to do with the sacrifices to the Lord were accomplished that day: the Passover was kept and the sacrifices were offered on the altar of the Lord, according to the command of King Josiah. And the people of Israel who were present at that time kept the Passover and the feast of unleavened bread seven days. No Passover like it had been kept in Israel since the times of Samuel the prophet; none of the kings of Israel had kept such a Passover as was kept by Josiah and the priests and Levites and the men of Judah and all of Israel who were dwelling in Jerusalem. In the eighteenth year of the reign of Josiah this Passover was kept.

And the deeds of Josiah were upright in the sight of the Lord, for his heart was full of godliness. The events of his reign have been recorded in the past, concerning those who sinned and acted wickedly toward the Lord beyond any other people or kingdom, and how they grieved the Lord deeply, so that the words of the Lord rose up against Israel. After all these acts of Josiah, it happened that Pharaoh, king of Egypt, went to make war at Carchemish on the Euphrates, and Josiah went out against him.

And the king of Egypt sent word to him saying, "What have we to do with each other, king of Judea? I was not sent against you by the Lord God, for my war is at the Euphrates. And now the Lord is with me! The Lord is with me, urging me on! Stand aside, and do not oppose the Lord." But Josiah did not turn back to his chariot, but tried to fight with him, and did not heed the words of Jeremiah the prophet from the mouth of the Lord.

5 Ezra

The second book of the prophet Ezra the son of Seraiah, son of Azariah, son of Hilkiah, son of Shallum, son of Zadok, son of Ahitub, son of Ahijah, son of Phinehas, son of Eli, son of Amariah, son of Azariah, son of Meraioth, son of Arna, son of Uzzi, son of Borith, son of Abishua, son of Phinehas, son of Eleazar, son of Aaron, of the tribe of Levi, who was a captive in the country of the Medes in the reign of Artaxerxes, king of the Persians.

The word of the Lord came to me, saying, "Go and declare to my people their evil deeds, and to their children the iniquities which they have committed against me, so that they may tell their children's children that the sins of their parents have increased in them, for they have forgotten me and have offered sacrifices to strange gods. Was it not I who brought them out of the land of Egypt, out of the house of bondage? But they have angered me and despised my counsels.

Pull out the hair of your head and hurl all evils upon them, for they have not obeyed my law -- they are a rebellious people. How long shall I endure them, on whom I have bestowed such great benefits? For their sake I have overthrown many kings: I struck down Pharaoh with his servants, and all his army. I have destroyed all nations before them, and scattered in the east the people of two provinces, Tyre and Sidon; I have slain all their enemies. But speak to them and say, Thus says the Lord: Surely it was I who brought you through the sea, and made safe highways for you where there was no road; I gave you Moses as leader and Aaron as priest; I provided light for you from a pillar of fire, and did great wonders among you. Yet you have forgotten me," says the Lord.

Thus says the Lord Almighty: "The quails were a sign to you; I gave you camps for your protection, and in them you complained. You have not exulted in my name at the destruction of your enemies, but to this day you still complain. Where are the benefits which I bestowed on you? When you were hungry and thirsty in the wilderness, did you not cry out to me, saying, 'Why hast thou led us into this wilderness to kill us? It would have been better for us to serve the Egyptians than to die in this wilderness.' I pitied your groanings and gave you manna for food; you ate the bread of angels.

When you were thirsty, did I not cleave the rock so that waters flowed in abundance? Because of the heat I covered you with the leaves of trees. I divided fertile lands among you; I drove out the Canaanites, the Perizzites, and the Philistines before you.

What more can I do for you?" says the Lord. Thus says the Lord Almighty: "When you were in the wilderness, at the bitter stream, thirsty and blaspheming my name, I did not send fire upon you for your blasphemies, but threw a tree into the water and made the stream sweet."

"What shall I do to you, O Jacob? You would not obey me, O Judah. I will turn to other nations and will give them my name, that they may keep my statutes. Because you have forsaken me, I also will forsake you. When you beg mercy of me, I will show you no mercy. When you call upon me, I will not listen to you; for you have defiled your hands with blood, and your feet are swift to commit murder. It is not as though you had forsaken me; you have forsaken yourselves," says the Lord.

Thus says the Lord Almighty: "Have I not entreated you as a father entreats his sons or a mother her daughters or a nurse her children, that you should be my people and I should be your God, and that you should be my sons and I should be your father? I gathered you as a hen gathers her brood under her wings. But now, what shall I do to you? I will cast you out from my presence."

6 Ezra

"Now concerning the signs: behold, the days are coming when those who dwell on earth shall be seized with great terror, and the way of truth shall be hidden, and the land shall be barren of faith. And unrighteousness shall be increased beyond what you yourself see, and beyond what you heard of formerly. And the land which you now see ruling shall be waste and untrod den, and men shall see it desolate. But if the Most High grants that you live, you shall see it thrown into confusion after the third period; and the sun shall suddenly shine forth at night, and the moon during the day. Blood shall drip from wood, and the stone shall utter its voice; the peoples shall be troubled, and the stars shall fall.

And one shall reign whom those who dwell on earth do not expect, and the birds shall fly away together; and the sea of Sodom shall cast up fish; and one whom the many do not know shall make his voice heard by night, and all shall hear his voice.

There shall be chaos also in many places, and fire shall often break out, and the wild beasts shall roam beyond their haunts, and menstruous women shall bring forth monsters. And salt waters shall be found in the sweet, and all friends shall conquer one another; then shall reason hide itself, and wisdom shall withdraw into its chamber, and it shall be sought by many but shall not be found, and unrighteousness and unrestraint shall increase on earth. And one country shall ask its neighbor, 'Has righteousness, or any one who does right, passed through you?' And it will answer, 'No.' And at that time men shall hope but not obtain; they shall labor but their ways shall not prosper.

These are the signs which I am permitted to tell you, and if you pray again, and weep as you do now, and fast for seven days, you shall hear yet greater things than these." Then I awoke, and my body shuddered violently, and my soul was so troubled that it fainted. But the angel who had come and talked with me held me and strengthened me and set me on my feet. Now on the second night Phaltiel, a chief of the people, came to me and said, "Where have you been? And why is your face sad? Or do you not know that Israel has been entrusted to you in the land of their exile? Rise therefore and eat some bread, so that you may not forsake us, like a shepherd who leaves his flock in the power of cruel wolves." Then I said to him, "Depart from me and do not come near me for seven days, and then you may come to me." He heard what I said and left me.

Then my soul recovered the spirit of understanding, and I began once more to speak words in the presence of the Most High. And I said, "O sovereign Lord, from every forest of the earth and from all its trees thou hast chosen one vine, and from all the lands of the world thou hast chosen for thyself one region, and from all the flowers of the world thou hast chosen for thyself one lily, and from all the depths of the sea thou hast filled for thyself one river, and from all the cities that have been built thou hast consecrated Zion for thyself, and from all the birds that have been created thou hast named for thyself one dove, and from all the flocks that have been made thou hast provided for thyself one sheep, and from all the multitude of peoples thou hast gotten for thyself one people; and to this people, whom thou hast loved, thou hast given the law which is approved by all.

And now, O Lord, why hast thou given over the one to the many, and dishonored the one root beyond the others, and scattered your only one among the many? And those who opposed thy promises have trodden down those who believed thy covenants. If thou do really hate thy people, they should be punished at thy own hands." When I had spoken these words, the angel who had come to me on a previous night was sent to me, and he said to me, "Listen to me, and I will instruct you; pay attention to me, and I will tell you more." And I said, "Speak, my lord." And he said to me, "Are you greatly disturbed in mind over Israel? Or do you love him more than his Maker does?" And I said, "No, my lord, but because of my grief I have spoken; for every hour I suffer agonies of heart, while I strive to understand the way of the Most High and to search out part of his judgment."

And he said to me, "You cannot." And I said, "Why not, my lord? Why then was I born? Or why did not my mother's womb become my grave, that I might not see the travail of Jacob and the exhaustion of the people of Israel?" He said to me, "I shall liken my judgment to a circle; just as for those who are last there is no slowness, so for those who are first there is no haste." Then I answered and said, "Couldst thou not have created at one time those who have been and those who are and those who will be, that thou mightest show thy judgment the sooner?" He replied to me and said, "The creation cannot make more haste than the Creator, neither can the world hold at one time those who have been created in it."

Psalms of Solomon

Love righteousness, you rulers of the earth, think of the Lord with uprightness, and seek him with sincerity of heart; because he is found by those who do not put him to the test, and manifests himself to those who do not distrust him. For perverse thoughts separate men from God, and when his power is tested, it convicts the foolish; because wisdom will not enter a deceitful soul, nor dwell in a body enslaved to sin. For a holy and disciplined spirit will flee from deceit, and will rise and depart from foolish thoughts, and will be ashamed at the approach of unrighteousness. For wisdom is a kindly spirit and will not free a blasphemer from the guilt of his words; because God is witness of his inmost feelings, and a true observer of his heart, and a hearer of his tongue.

Because the Spirit of the Lord has filled the world, and that which holds all things together knows what is said; therefore no one who utters unrighteous things will escape notice, and justice, when it punishes, will not pass him by. For inquiry will be made into the counsels of an ungodly man, and a report of his words will come to the Lord, to convict him of his lawless deeds; because a jealous ear hears all things, and the sound of murmurings does not go unheard.

Beware then of useless murmuring, and keep your tongue from slander; because no secret word is without result, and a lying mouth destroys the soul. Do not invite death by the error of your life, nor bring on destruction by the works of your hands; because God did not make death, and he does not delight in the death of the living. For he created all things that they might exist, and the generative forces of the world are wholesome, and there is no destructive poison in them; and the dominion of Hades is not on earth. For righteousness is immortal. But ungodly men by their words and deeds summoned death; considering him a friend, they pined away, and they made a covenant with him, because they are fit to belong to his party.

But the souls of the righteous are in the hand of God, and no torment will ever touch them. In the eyes of the foolish they seemed to have died, and their departure was thought to be an affliction, and their going from us to be their destruction; but they are at peace. For though in the sight of men they were punished, their hope is full of immortality. Having been disciplined a little, they will receive great good, because God tested them and found them worthy of himself; like gold in the furnace he tried them, and like a sacrificial burnt offering he accepted them. In the time of their visitation they will shine forth, and will run like sparks through the stubble. They will govern nations and rule over peoples, and the Lord will reign over them for ever.

Those who trust in him will understand truth, and the faithful will abide with him in love, because grace and mercy are upon his elect, and he watches over his holy ones. But the ungodly will be punished as their reasoning deserves, who disregarded the righteous man and rebelled against the Lord; for whoever despises wisdom and instruction is miserable. Their hope is vain, their labors are unprofitable, and their works are useless. Their wives are foolish, and their children evil; their offspring are accursed. For blessed is the barren woman who is undefiled, who has not entered into a sinful union; she will have fruit when God examines souls.

I also am mortal, like all men, a descendant of the first-formed child of earth; and in the womb of a mother I was molded into flesh, within the period of ten months, compacted with blood, from the seed of a man and the pleasure of marriage. And when I was born, I began to breathe the common air, and fell upon the kindred earth, and my first sound was a cry, like that of all. I was nursed with care in swaddling cloths. For no king has had a different beginning of existence; there is for all mankind one entrance into life, and a common departure.

Therefore I prayed, and understanding was given me; I called upon God, and the spirit of wisdom came to me. I preferred her to scepters and thrones, and I accounted wealth as nothing in comparison with her. Neither did I liken to her any priceless gem, because all gold is but a little sand in her sight, and silver will be accounted as clay before her. I loved her more than health and beauty, and I chose to have her rather than light, because her radiance never ceases. All good things came to me along with her, and in her hands uncounted wealth.

I rejoiced in them all, because wisdom leads them; but I did not know that she was their mother. I learned without guile and I impart without grudging; I do not hide her wealth, for it is an unfailing treasure for men; those who get it obtain friendship with God, commended for the gifts that come from instruction. May God grant that I speak with judgment and have thought worthy of what I have received, for he is the guide even of wisdom and the corrector of the wise.

Odes of Solomon

No man, O my God, changeth thy holy place. And it is not possible that he should change it and put it in another place because he hath no power over it. For thy sanctuary thou hast designed before thou didst make other places. That which is the elder shall not be altered by those that are younger than itself. Thou has given thy heart, O Lord, to thy believers. Never wilt thou fail, nor be without fruits. For one hour of thy Faith is days and years. For who is there put on thy grace, and be hurt? For thy seal is known, and thy creatures know it, and thy heavenly hosts possess it, and the elect archangels are clad with it. Thou hast given us thy fellowship. It was not that thou wast in need of us, but that we are in need of thee. Distill thy dews upon us and open thy rich fountains that pour forth to us milk and honey. For there is no repentance with thee that thou shouldest repent of anything that thou hast promised. And the end was revealed before thee. For what thou gavest, thou gavest freely. So that thou mayest not draw them back and take them again. For all was revealed before thee as God, and ordered from the beginning before thee. And thou, O God, hast made all things. Hallelujah.

I will give thanks unto thee, O Lord, because I love thee. O Most High, thou wilt not forsake me for thou art my hope. Freely I have received thy grace, I shall live thereby. My persecutors will come and not see me. A cloud of darkness shall fall on their eyes; and an air of thick gloom shall darken them. And they shall have no light to see; they may not take hold upon me. Let their counsel become thick darkness, and what they have cunningly devised, let it return upon their own heads. For they have devised a counsel and it did not succeed. For my hope is upon the Lord and I will not fear, and because the Lord is my salvation, I will not fear. And He is a garland on my head and I shall not be moved; even if everything should be shaken, I stand firm. And if all things visible should perish, I shall not die; because the Lord is with me and I am with Him. Hallelujah.

As the hand moves over the harp, and the strings speak, so speaks in my members the Spirit of the Lord, and I speak by His love. For it destroys what is foreign and everything that is bitter. For thus it was from the beginning and will be to the end, that nothing should be His adversary, and nothing should stand up against Him. The Lord has multiplied the knowledge of Himself, and is zealous that these things should be known, which by His grace have been given to us. And the praise of His name He gave us; our spirits praise His holy Spirit. For there went forth a stream and became a river great and broad. For it flooded and broke up everything and it brought water to the

Temple. And the restrainers of the children of men were not able to restrain it, nor the arts of those whose business it is to restrain waters.

For it spread over the face of the whole earth, and filled everything; and all the thirsty upon earth were given to drink of it. And thirst was relieved and quenched; for from the Most High the draught was given. Blessed then are the ministers of that draught who are entrusted with that water. They have assuaged the dry lips, and the will that had fainted they have raised up. And souls that were near departing they have caught back from death. And limbs that had fallen they straightened and set up. They gave strength for their feebleness and light to their eyes. For everyone knew them in the Lord, and they lived by the water of life forever. Hallelujah.

As the impulse of anger against evil, so is the impulse of joy over what is lovely, and brings in of its fruits without restraint. My joy is the Lord and my impulse is toward Him; this path of mine is excellent. For I have a helper, the Lord. He hath caused me to know Himself, without grudging, by His simplicity. His kindness has humbled His greatness. He became like me, in order that I might receive Him. He was reckoned like myself in order that I might put Him on. And I trembled not when I saw Him because He was gracious to me. Like my nature He became that I might learn Him and like my form, that I might not turn back from Him. The Father of knowledge is the word of knowledge. He who created wisdom is wiser than His works. And He who created me when yet I was not knew what I should do when I came into being.

Wherefore He pitied me in His abundant grace and granted me to ask from Him and to receive from His sacrifice. Because He it is that is incorrupt, the fullness of the ages and the of them. He hath given Him to be seen of them that are His, in order that they may recognize Him that made them, and that they might not suppose that they came of themselves. For knowledge He hath appointed as its way, hath widened it and extended it; and brought to all perfection. And set over it the traces of His light, and I walked therein from the beginning even to the end. For by Him it was wrought, and He was resting in the Son, and for its salvation He will take hold of everything. And the Most High shall be known in His Saints, to announce to those that have songs of the coming of the Lord.

That they may go forth to meet Him, and may sing to Him with joy and with the harp of many tones. The seers shall come before Him and they shall be seen before Him. And they shall praise the Lord for His love; because He is near and beholdeth. And hatred shall be taken from the earth, and along with jealousy it shall be drowned. For ignorance hath been destroyed, because the knowledge of the Lord hath arrived.

They who make songs shall sing the grace of the Lord Most High. And they shall bring their songs, and their heart shall be like the day; and like the excellent beauty of the Lord their pleasant song. And there shall neither be anything that breathes without knowledge nor any that is dumb. For He hath given a mouth to His creation, to open the voice of the mouth towards Him, to praise Him. Confess ye His power, and show forth His grace. Hallelujah.

Letter of Aristeas

Philokratés, a noteworthy narrative has been compiled of a meeting which we had with Eleazar, the chief-priest of the Judeans, arising from the great importance which you attached to hearing a personal account of our mission, its content and purpose. By detailing each aspect I have tried to present you a clear exposition of it, realizing your love-of-learning, which is a great quality in any human who has tried continually to increase his learning and understanding, whether from the histories of others or even by actual experience. For it is by this means, by the attainment of the most beautiful ends, that the soul is furnished with a clean disposition; and which, by having fixed its aim on the piety (the highest of all ends), lives by adopting an infallible rule.

We have the set purpose, which is devoted to the special study of the things of God, and offered ourselves as a body of elders to the previously-mentioned man, whose conduct and glory have won him preeminent-honor in the eyes of both citizens and others alike. And he has gained the greatest benefits for those with him and for the citizens in other places, by his interpretation of the divine law, due to it having been written by them on parchments in Hebraic characters. We also undertook this task with enthusiasm, seizing an opportunity with the king in connection with those who were transported to Egypt from Judah by the king his father, who was both the original founder of the city and took over Egypt. It is worthwhile telling you this as well, for I am convinced that because you are more favorably inclined toward the solemnity and the disposition of the humans who live by the solemn law, concerning whom we propose to write, you will gladly listen, since you have paid a fresh visit to us from your island, and wish to hear with us of matters pertaining to edification of the soul.

Now I had also previously sent you the record of what I regarded as the most noteworthy matters. We received this record of the race of the Judeans from the most eloquent chief-priests in eloquent Egypt. For since you have such a love-of-learning concerning things which are beneficial to the mind, it is indeed my duty to share this with all like-minded persons, but all the more so with you, for you have a kindred inclination, being not only a natural brother in character, but instead also in the pursuit of beauty the same as we are. For the value of gold or any other treasure among those honored by the empty-headed does not possess the same value, as compared with the pursuit of discipline and the care about these things. But lest we prolong the introduction, indulging in idle chatter, we will proceed to the main part of the narrative.

But also regarding the copy of the command, I think that its insertion will be not unprofitable. For the king's magnificence will also be more clearly manifested by it, as God gives him strength to bring this salvation to vast multitudes. Now it was as follows: By order of the king: everyone who served our father's expeditions in the regions of Syria and Phoiniké, and who, in their advance upon the country of the Judeans, became masters of any Judean bodies whom they transported into either the city or the country, or sold to someone else (but also, any such captives who were there prior to the advance or were subsequently brought in): anyone who holds such persons are required to release them at once, receiving twenty drachmas as the price per individual. Indeed, in the case of soldiers, such money will be added to their salaries; but in the case of the remainder, from the royal bank.

For we believe, that these prisoners were taken contrary to our father's will, and in a manner against all fairness; but, that both the destruction of their country, and the transportation of the Judeans into Egypt, was a hasty act of military rashness. For the spoil which fell to the soldiers along the plain was sufficient for them. For this reason, the enslavement of these humans is absolutely unreasonable. Therefore, we have a reputation of dispensing righteousness to all humans, but, all the more, to those who are enslaved without good reason; and our overall aim is to promote both the righteousness and the piety in all things. Therefore, we have ordered that all Judean bodies in slavery everywhere in the kingdom, for whatever reason, shall be released, and that their owners receive the payment laid down above, and that no one shall act leisurely in these matters. But within three days following the publication of this command, the owners shall furnish registers of slaves to those appointed over these matters, and give immediate details of these individuals. For we have also concluded, that it is in the interest of ourselves and our affairs that this matter shall be accomplished. But anyone who wishes may bring a message to me concerning those who refuse to be compliant, on the understanding that he will assume the office of the accused if he was shown to be liable; but the possessions of such men shall be appropriated into the royal bank.

For you must not take the contemptible rationalization, that Moses enacted this legislation because of an excessive preoccupation with mice and weasels or suchlike creatures. Instead, everything has been solemnly set in order for pure investigation and amendment of conduct for the sake of righteousness. For the birds which we use are all domesticated and of exceptional cleanliness, their food consisting of wheat and pulse— such birds as pigeons, turtledoves, moorfowls, partridges, but, in addition, geese and others of the same kind.

But concerning the birds which are forbidden, you will find both savage and carnivorous kinds, and the rest which dominate over others by their own power, and who find their food by preying upon the previously-stated domesticated birds—which is an unrighteous-deed. But not only that, they instead, also seize lambs and kids, but even injure humans both dead and alive.

Therefore, by calling them unclean, he has thereby indicated that it is the solemn binding duty of those, for whom the legislation has been established, to practice righteousness in their soul, and not to lord it over anyone in reliance upon their own power, nor to deprive him of anything. Instead he has indicated that they are to steer their lives righteously, in the manner of the domesticated creatures among the previously-stated birds, which feed on those plants which grow on the ground and do not exercise a domination leading to the destruction either of those beneath them or of their own kind. By means of creatures like this, the lawgiver has handed down the lesson to be noted by men of intelligence, that they should both be righteous, and not achieve anything by force, nor dominate over others in reliance on their own strength. For since it is not even proper to touch any of the previously-stated creatures because of their particular habits, should not all possible precautions be taken to prevent our own courses from degenerating to their level?

Now the man who has been separated from the previously-stated way, is the man who is characterized as possessing the gift of memory. For example, all creatures that are cloven-footed and ruminate represent, to those who perceive it, the phenomenon of memory. For the rumination is nothing but the recalling of one's life and sustenance. For one's life is usually sustained by food.

For this reason, we are exhorted through the writings by the one who says the following, 'You shall remember the Lord, who did great and marvelous deeds in you.' For when they are properly understood they are manifestly great and glorious. Indeed, first, there is the construction of the body, and the digestion of the food, and the specific function connected with each limb. But much more, the orderly arrangement of the senses, the operation and unseen activity of the mind, and the speed of its reaction to each stimulus and its discovery of arts involves an infinite variety of methods. For this reason, he exhorts us to remember how the previously-stated blessings are preserved by a divine power under his preparation. For he has ordained every time and place to be a continual reminder of the God who is ruler and preserver of all.

Now on the following day, the same arrangement was made, and when the king deemed it an appropriate time to ask the men questions, he asked the first of those who had been left over for subsequent questioning, "What is the strongest form of government?"

Now he declared, "Control of oneself, and not being carried away by one's impulses. For all humans possess a certain natural bent of their mind in one direction or another. Indeed, the majority of men are likely to incline toward food and drink and pleasure, but the kings toward acquisition of a country, depending on the greatness of their glory. Yet, in everyone, moderation is a beautiful thing. But what God gives you, take and keep; but do not covet what is beyond your reach." Now the king, pleased with this reply, spoke to the next guest, "How could a man be free from envy?" Now after a pause, he declared, "First of all, by realizing that God assigns both glory and greatness of wealth to the kings, each and every one, and no one is a king by his own power. For all men wish to share this glory, but instead they cannot—for it is a gift of God." Now the king, after giving a long commendation to this guest, asked another, "How can a man despise his enemies?" Now he spoke, "By practicing goodwill to all humans and by forming friendships, you would owe no obligation to anyone. But to have gratitude with all humans, and to receive a handsome gift from God—this is one of the strongest gifts." Now the king, after approving these words, directed the next guest to answer, speaking to him, "How can a man maintain the glory he received?" Now he spoke, "If by his earnestness and his favors he showed munificence and great-generosity toward others, he would never lack glory. But if you wish for these previously-mentioned qualities to abide with you, you must call on God continually."

Now on the following day, the king seized the opportunity, asking the next guest, "What is the worst type of neglect?" He declared, "If a man is neglectful of his children, and does not devote every endeavor to bringing them up. For we are continually praying to God for ourselves as for our descendents, that every good-thing may rest upon them. But our petition that our little-ones may have some soundness-of-mind is something which comes to pass only by a power of God." Now the king, after declaring that he had spoken well, asked another guest, "How can a man be a lover-of-his-fatherland?" He spoke, "By adopting the view that it is a beautiful thing to live and to come-to-an-end in one's own country. But residence abroad indeed produces contempt upon the poor, but disgrace upon the rich, as though they had been exiled for evilness.

Therefore, by doing good to all, while you continually carry out this policy, you will undoubtedly be a lover-of-your-fatherland, God giving you favor in the sight of all." Now the king, after hearing this man, asked the next in order, "How can a man reach agreement with a woman?" He declared, "Indeed, by recognizing that the female gender is insolent, and drastic in the pursuit of what they wish to have, and that they are easily liable to sudden changes of opinion through fallacious-rationalization, and their nature is furnished weak. But it is necessary to have dealings with them in a sound way, and not to seek provocation which may lead to rivalry. For life prospers when the helmsman knows the goal toward which he ought to direct his course.

But it is only by calling on the help of God that a man can steer a true course of life at all times." Now the king, after giving assent to this man, asked the next guest, "How can a man be free from sin?" Now he declared, "By also doing everything with rationalization, and by not being persuaded by slanders. Instead, you must be your own examiner of what is said, and by your own judgment, decide the petitions which are made to you, and through your judgment bringing them to pass—that is how you would be free from sin, O king. But to have these intentions and to conduct oneself in the light of them is a work involving a divine power."

2 Baruch (Syriac Apocalypse)

These are the words of the book which Baruch the son of Neraiah, son of Mahseiah, son of Zedekiah, son of Hasadiah, son of Hilkiah, wrote in Babylon, in the fifth year, on the seventh day of the month, at the time when the Chaldeans took Jerusalem and burned it with fire. And Baruch read the words of this book in the hearing of Jeconiah the son of Jehoiakim, king of Judah, and in the hearing of all the people who came to hear the book, and in the hearing of the mighty men and the princes, and in the hearing of the elders, and in the hearing of all the people, small and great, all who dwelt in Babylon by the river Sud.

Then they wept, and fasted, and prayed before the Lord; and they collected money, each giving what he could; and they sent it to Jerusalem to Jehoiakim the high priest, the son of Hilkiah, son of Shallum, and to the priests, and to all the people who were present with him in Jerusalem. At the same time, on the tenth day of Sivan, Baruch took the vessels of the house of the Lord, which had been carried away from the temple, to return them to the land of Judah -- the silver vessels which Zedekiah the son of Josiah, king of Judah, had made, after Nebuchadnezzar king of Babylon had carried away from Jerusalem Jeconiah and the princes and the prisoners and the mighty men and the people of the land, and brought them to Babylon.

And they said: "Herewith we send you money; so buy with the money burnt offerings and sin offerings and incense, and prepare a cereal offering, and offer them upon the altar of the Lord our God; and pray for the life of Nebuchadnezzar king of Babylon, and for the life of Belshazzar his son, that their days on earth may be like the days of heaven. And the Lord will give us strength, and he will give light to our eyes, and we shall live under the protection of Nebuchadnezzar king of Babylon, and under the protection of Belshazzar his son, and we shall serve them many days and find favor in their sight. And pray for us to the Lord our God, for we have sinned against the Lord our God, and to this day the anger of the Lord and his wrath have not turned away from us.

And you shall read this book which we are sending you, to make your confession in the house of the Lord on the days of the feasts and at appointed seasons. And you shall say: Righteousness belongs to the Lord our God, but confusion of face, as at this day, to us, to the men of Judah, to the inhabitants of Jerusalem, and to our kings and our princes and our priests and our prophets and our fathers, because we have sinned before the Lord, and have disobeyed him, and have not heeded the voice of the Lord our God, to walk in the statutes of the Lord which he set before us.

From the day when the Lord brought our fathers out of the land of Egypt until today, we have been disobedient to the Lord our God, and we have been negligent, in not heeding his voice.

So to this day there have clung to us the calamities and the curse which the Lord declared through Moses his servant at the time when he brought our fathers out of the land of Egypt to give to us a land flowing with milk and honey. We did not heed the voice of the Lord our God in all the words of the prophets whom he sent to us, but we each followed the intent of his own wicked heart by serving other gods and doing what is evil in the sight of the Lord our God."

3 Baruch (Greek Apocalypse)

A narrative and revelation of Baruch, concerning those ineffable things which he saw by command of God. Bless Thou, O Lord.

A revelation of Baruch, who stood upon the river Gel weeping over the captivity of Jerusalem, when also Abimelech was preserved by the hand of God, at the farm of Agrippa. And he was sitting thus at the beautiful gates, where the Holy of holies lay.

Verily I Baruch was weeping in my mind and sorrowing on account of the people, and that Nebuchadnezzar the king was permitted by God to destroy His city, saying: "Lord, why didst Thou set on fire Thy vineyard, and lay it waste? Why didst Thou do this? And why, Lord, didst Thou not requite us with another chastiscment, but didst deliver us to nations such as these, so that they reproach us and say, Where is their God?" And behold as I was weeping and saying such things, I saw an angel of the Lord coming and saying to me: "Understand, O man, greatly beloved, and trouble not thyself so greatly concerning the salvation of Jerusalem, for thus saith the Lord God, the Almighty. For He sent me before thee, to make known and to show to thee all the things of God. For thy prayer was heard before Him, and entered into the ears of the Lord God." And when he had said these things to me, I was silent. And the angel said to me: "Cease to provoke God, and I will show thee other mysteries, greater than these." And I Baruch said, As the Lord God liveth, if thou wilt show me, and I hear a word of thine, I will not continue to speak any longer. God shall add to my judgement in the day of judgement, if I speak hereafter. And the angel of the powers said to me, "Come, and I will show thee the mysteries of God."

And he took me and led me where the firmament has been set fast, and where there was a river which no one can cross, nor any strange breeze of all those which God created. And he took me and led me to the first heaven, and showed me a door of great size. And he said to me, "Let us enter through it, and we entered as though borne on wings, a distance of about thirty days journey." And he showed me within the heaven a plain; and there were men dwelling thereon, with the faces of oxen, and the horns of stags and the feet of goats, and the haunches of lambs. And I Baruch asked the angel, "Make known to me, I pray thee, what is the thickness of the heaven in which we journeyed, or what is its extent, or what is the plain, in order that I may also tell the sons of men?"

And the angel whose name is Phamael said to me: "This door which thou seest is the door of heaven, and as great as is the distance from earth to heaven, so great also is its thickness; and again as great as is the distance from North to South, so great is the length of the plain which thou didst see." And again the angel of the powers said to me, "Come, and I will show thee greater mysteries."

But I said, "I pray thee show me what are these men." And he said to me, "These are they who built the tower of strife against God, and the Lord banished them."

And the angel of the Lord took me and led me to a second heaven. And he showed me there also a door like the first and said, "Let us enter through it." And we entered, being borne on wings a distance of about sixty days journey. And he showed me there also a plain, and it was full of men, whose appearance was like that of dogs, and whose feet were like those of stags. And I asked the angel: "I pray thee, Lord, say to me who are these." And he said, "These are they who gave counsel to build the tower, for they whom thou seest drove forth multitudes of both men and women, to make bricks; among whom, a woman making bricks was not allowed to be released in the hour of child-birth, but brought forth while she was making bricks, and carried her child in her apron, and continued to make bricks. And the Lord appeared to them and confused their speech, when they had built the tower to the height of four hundred and sixty-three cubits. And they took a gimlet, and sought to pierce the heaven, saying, 'Let us see whether the heaven is made of clay, or of brass, or of iron.' When God saw this He did not permit them, but smote them with blindness and confusion of speech, and rendered them as thou seest."

And I Baruch said, "Behold, Lord, Thou didst show me great and wonderful things; and now show me all things for the sake of the Lord." And the angel said to me, "Come, let us proceed." And I proceeded with the angel from that place about one hundred and eighty-five days journey. And he showed me a plain and a serpent, which appeared to be two hundred plethra in length. And he showed me Hades, and its appearance was dark and abominable. And I said, "Who is this dragon, and who is this monster around him?" And the angel said, "The dragon is he who eats the bodies of those who spend their life wickedly, and he is nourished by them. And this is Hades, which itself also closely resembles him, in that it also drinks about a cubit from the sea, which does not sink at all." And I Baruch said, "And how does this happen?" And the angel said, "Hearken, the Lord God made three hundred and sixty rivers, of which the chief of all are Alphias, Abyrus, and the Gericus; and because of these the sea does not sink." And I said, "I pray thee show me which is the tree which led Adam astray."

And the angel said to me, "It is the vine, which the angel Sammael planted, whereat the Lord God was angry, and He cursed him and his plant, while also on this account He did not permit Adam to touch it, and therefore the devil being envious deceived him through his vine." And I Baruch said, "Since also the vine has been the cause of such great evil, and is under judgment of the curse of God, and was the destruction of the first created, how is it now so useful?" And the angel said, "Thou askest aright.

When God caused the deluge upon earth, and destroyed all flesh, and four hundred and nine thousand giants, and the water rose fifteen cubits above the highest mountains, then the water entered into paradise and destroyed every flower; but it removed wholly without the bounds the shoot of the vine and cast it outside. And when the earth appeared out of the water, and Noah came out of the ark, he began to plant of the plants which he found. But he found also the shoot of the vine; and he took it, and was reasoning in himself, 'What then is it?' And I came and spake to him the things concerning it. And he said, 'Shall I plant it, or what shall I do? Since Adam was destroyed because of it, let me not also meet with the anger of God because of it.' And saying these things he prayed that God would reveal to him what he should do concerning it. And when he had completed the prayer which lasted forty days, and having besought many things and wept, he said: 'Lord, I entreat thee to reveal to me what I shall do concerning this plant.' But God sent his angel Sarasael, and said to him, 'Arise, Noah, and plant the shoot of the vine, for thus saith the Lord: Its bitterness shall be changed into sweetness, and its curse shall become a blessing, and that which is produced from it shall become the blood of God.' And as through it the human race obtained condemnation, so again through Jesus Christ the Immanuel will they receive in Him the upward calling, and the entry into paradise."

4 Ezra

And it gave thee Adam, a dead body, and he was the formation of thy hands; and thou didst breathe in him the breath of life and he was living before thee; and thou leddest him into Paradise which thy right hand did plant before ever the earth came. And to this one thou didst give the commandment, and he transgressed it and forthwith thou didst decree upon him death, and upon his generations. And from him were born peoples and tribes and tongues and clans which are without number.

And all peoples followed their own works, and dealt wickedly and were ungodly before thee— and thou didst not hinder them. But again in due time thou didst bring the Flood upon the earth and upon the inhabitants of the world, and thou didst destroy them; and their destruction was alike, and as to Adam came death, so to them came the death Of the Flood.

Nevertheless thou didst spare one of them with his household— and from him all the righteous are descended. And it came to pass when the inhabitants of the earth began to multiply, and multiplied children and peoples and many multitudes, and began again to be ungodly more than the former generations, it came to pass that when they practised ungodliness before thee, thou didst choose one of them for thyself, whose name was Abraham; and thou didst love him, and thou didst show him the consummation of the times, him alone, between thee and him by night; and thou didst establish with him an everlasting covenant, and didst promise him that thou wouldest never forsake his seed.

And thou gavest him Isaac, and to Isaac thou gavest Jacob and Esau; and thou didst choose thee Jacob for an heritage, and Esau thou didst hate; and Jacob became a great people. And when thou didst bring up his seed from Egypt and didst establish with him an everlasting covenant, and didst bring them to Mount Sinai, Thou didst incline the heavens, and didst shake the earth and madest the world quake, and caused the deeps to tremble, and didst alarm the worlds. And thy glory went through the four gates of fire and earthquake, and Of wind and cold, that thou mightest give to Jacob's seed the Law, and to the race of Israel commandments. And yet thou didst not remove from them the evil heart, that thy Law might yield fruit in them.

For the first Adam clothed himself with the evil heart, and transgressed, and was overcome (and not only so) but also all who were begotten from him. And the infirmity remained in them, and also the Law, together with the evil root; then what was good departed, and the evil came. And the times passed away, and the seasons were ended; and thou didst raise up for thyself a servant whose name was David;

and thou commandedst him to build a city for thy name [and a House] that oblations from thine own might be offered there in. And this was done many years.

But the inhabitants of the City sinned against thee and did nothing new beyond what Adam had done and all his generations for they also were clothing themselves with the evil heart. And so thou deliveredst thy City into the hand Of thine enemies. And when I heard these things I fell upon my face and said to him: "It would have been better for us if we had not come than, having come, that we should live in sin and suffer, and not know why we suffer.

Come, let us go and make war with the sea that it may recede before us, and we will make us more woods." The waves of the sea likewise deliberated together, and said: "Come let us go up and wage war with the wood of the plain in order that there we make us another place." And the deliberation of the wood was in vain, for the fire came and consumed it; and likewise also the deliberation of the waves of the sea, for the sand stood up and stopped them. "If then thou hadst been judge of these, which of them wouldest thou have acquitted, and which of them wouldest thou have condemned?" And I answered and said: "Both of them have deliberated a vain deliberation; for the land hath been given to the Wood, and the place of the sea to bear its waves." And I answered and said: "How long and when shall these things be? For few and evil are our years."

And he answered and said to me: "Thou mayest not hasten more than the Most High; for thou art hastening for thine own self, but the Most High for the sake Of many. For did not the souls of the righteous ask concerning these things in their chambers, and say: How long shall we be here? And when cometh the harvest Of our reward? And the angel Remiel answered and said to them: Until the number of those like you be fulfilled."

The Shepherd of Hermas

The man who nourished me has sold me to a certain Rhodé into Roma. Many years after this, I saw her and I wished that I would make myself known to her again and I began to be loving her as a sister. After some time, I saw her while she was bathing herself into the river, the Tiber, and I gave my hand to her, and I led her out of the river. Therefore, after I saw the beauty of this woman, I was thoroughly rationalizing in my heart, saying, "How happy I would be if I was having such a woman and one with her beauty and her manner!" I deliberated with myself only this thought; but another thought, not even one.

After some time, while I was going into the countryside, and while I was glorifying the creations of God (about how great and remarkable and powerful they are), I fell into slumber while walking around. And a spirit took me and brought me away through a certain roadless region, through which a human was not being able to make his way. But the place was precipitous and having been ripped off from the waters. Therefore, after I crossed through that river, I came into level areas. And I put my knees on the ground, and I began to be praying to the Lord and to be confessing forth my sins.

But while I was praying to the Lord, the heaven was opened up, and I looked at that woman whom I desired, greeting me out of the heaven, saying, "Be rejoicing, Hermas!" But after I looked at her, I said to her, "Lady, what are you doing here?" But she answered me, "I was taken up in order that I might convict you of your sins with the Lord." I said to her, "Are you to convict me right now?" "No," she declared. "Instead, hear the words which I am going to be saying to you. The god, the one who is residing in the heavens, and who created the things which are out of the thing which is not, and who multiplied and grew them for the sake of his holy assembly, is being angered with you because you sinned against me." I answered her and said, "Sinned against you? How so? Or at what time did I utter a shameful word to you? Did I not always esteem you as a goddess? Did I not always respect you as a sister? Woman, why are you falsely charging me with these wicked and unclean things?"

After she laughed at me, she said, "The desire of that wickedness did ascend upon your heart. Or are you not thinking it to be a wicked matter, if at any time the wicked desire might ascend upon the heart of a righteous man? Yet it is a sin, even a great sin," she declared. "For the righteous man deliberates with himself about what is righteous. Therefore, in the act for him to be deliberating with himself righteous things, his glory is setting itself straight in the heavens, and he has the Lord placable in every affair of his.

But the ones who are deliberating with themselves wicked things in their hearts, are drawing death and captivity on to themselves, especially the ones who are acquiring this age and are prancing in their riches and are not holding themselves to the good things, the things which are going to come. Their souls will change their mind, whichever ones have no hope in the Lord. Instead, they have despaired of them and their life.

Instead, you be praying to God, and he will heal the sinful actions of you and of your whole house and of all the holy ones."

After the event for her to utter these words, the heavens were locked. And I was totally shuddering and grieving. But I was saying in myself, "If even this sin is written up against me, how will I be able to be saved? Or how will I make atonement to the Lord God about my many sins, my complete sins? Or with what kind of words might I ask the Lord in order that he might be gracious to me?"

As I was taking counsel and discerning these things in my heart, I looked at a great white seat for reclining, standing opposite me, made out of snow-white wool, like snow. And a woman, an elderly lady dressed in brightest apparel, came, having a book in her hand. And she sat down alone, and she greeted me, "Be rejoicing, Hermas!" And I, grieving and weeping, spoke to her, "Be rejoicing, lady!"

And she spoke to me, "Why are you so sullen, Hermas? Why is the long-suffering and not-easily-upset one, the always laughing one, so downcast in his appearance and not cheerful?" And I spoke to her, "By a most good woman saying, that I sinned against her." But she was declaring, "Far be such a matter from the slave of God. Instead, a desire about her surely ascended upon your heart. Indeed, a deliberation such as this brings a sin upon the slaves of God. For it is a wicked and horrible deliberation against an all-solemn spirit, and within one which has already been proved, if at any time it might desire a wicked work, and especially when that spirit is Hermas, the self-restrained, the one who is distancing himself from every wicked desire and is full of all simplicity and a great lack of evil.

Instead, this is not the reason why God is being angered with you. Instead, it is in order that you might turn around your house which acted lawlessly against the Lord and against both of you, their parents. Instead, because you are fond of your children, you were not admonishing them; instead, you permitted them to be terribly destroyed. Due to this, the Lord is being angered with you. Instead, he will heal all the wicked deeds which have previously come to be in your house. For it is because of their sins and lawless deeds that you were destroyed by your mundane acts.

51

Instead, the abundant compassion of the Lord had mercy on you and on your house, and he will make you strong and will found you in his glory. Only may you not become lazy; instead, be being of a good soul, and be making your house strong. For as a bronze-smith, by hammering his work, obtains mastery of it for whatever affair he wants, so also does the account, the daily one, the righteous one, obtain mastery of all wickedness. Therefore, may you not stop admonishing your children; for I have come to know, that if at any time they will change their mind out of a whole heart of theirs, they will be enrolled into the books of the life with the holy ones."

After the event for these words of hers to be ceased, she said to me, "Do you want to hear me read aloud?" And I said, "I want to, lady." She said to me, "Become a hearer, and be hearing the glories of God."

The Testaments of the Twelve Patriarchs

The Testaments of the Twelve Patriarchs of the House of Israel is the collected words of the twelve sons of Jacob which they spoke to their children. Their testaments have been passed down throughout the generations of their posterity. In these testaments, the Patriarchs of Israel recount the events that shaped their lives and leave their posterity instruction, to love God and keep His Commandments. Their father Jacob had gathered his sons at the time of his death to bless and instruct them as well.

The Blessings of Jacob in Genesis "And Jacob called to his sons, and said, "Gather yourselves together, that I may tell you that which shall befall you in the last days. Gather yourselves together, and hear, you sons of Jacob; and hearken unto Israel, your father. Reuben, you are my firstborn, my might, and the beginning of my strength, the excellency of dignity, and the excellency of power. Unstable as water, you shall not excel; because you went up to your father's bed; then you defiled it: he went up to my couch.

Simeon and Levi are brethren; instruments of cruelty are in their habitations. O my soul, come not into their secret; unto their assembly, mine honor, be not united: for in their anger they slew a man, and in their self-will they digged down a wall. Cursed be their anger, for it was fierce; and their wrath, for it was cruel: I will divide them in Jacob, and scatter them in Israel.

Judah, you are he whom your brethren shall praise: your hand shall be in the neck of your enemies; your father's children shall bow down before you. Judah is a lion's whelp: from the prey, my son, you are gone up: he stooped down, he couched as a lion, and as an old lion; who shall rouse him up? The sceptre shall not depart from Judah, nor a lawgiver from between his feet, until he comes whose right it is to reign; and unto him shall the gathering of the people be.

Zebulun shall dwell at the haven of the sea and he shall be for a haven of ships; and his border shall be unto Zidon.

Issachar is a strong ass couching down between two burdens: And he saw that rest was good, and the land that it was pleasant; and bowed his shoulder to bear, and became a servant unto tribute.

Dan shall judge his people, as one of the tribes of Israel. Dan shall be a serpent by the way, an adder in the path, that bites the horse heels, so that his rider shall fall backward. I have waited for Your salvation, O Lord.

Gad, a troop shall overcome him: but he shall overcome at the last.

Out of Asher his bread shall be fat, and he shall yield royal dainties.

Naphtali is a hind let loose: he gives goodly words.

Joseph is a fruitful bough, even a fruitful bough by a well; whose branches run over the wall: The archers have sorely grieved him, and shot at him, and hated him: But his bow abode in strength, and the arms of his hands were made strong by the hands of the mighty God of Jacob; (from thence is the shepherd, the stone of Israel) Even by the God of your father, who shall help you; and by the Almighty, who shall bless you with blessings of heaven above, blessings of the deep that lies under, blessings of the breasts, and of the womb: The blessings of your father have prevailed above the blessings of my progenitors unto the utmost bound of the everlasting hills: they shall be on the head of Joseph, and on the crown of the head of him that was separated from his brethren.

Benjamin shall ravin as a wolf: in the morning he shall devour the prey, and at night he shall divide the spoil."

All these are the twelve tribes of Israel: and this is it that which their father spoke to them, and blessed them; every one.

The Testament of Adam

And after three days, while I am in the tomb, I will raise up the body I received from you. And I will set you at the right hand of my divinity, and I will make you a god just like you wanted. And I will receive favor from God, and I will restore to you and to your posterity that which is the justice of heaven. "You have heard, my son Seth, that a Flood is coming and will wash the whole earth because of the daughters of Cain, your brother, who killed your brother Abel out of passion for your sister Lebuda, since sins had been created through your mother, Eve. And after the Flood there will be six thousand years left to the form of the world, and then its end will come." The heavenly powers: what they are like and how each of their orders is occupied in the service and the plan of this world. Listen, my beloved, as they are set in order one after another from the bottom, until we reach those who carry our Lord Jesus the Messiah and bear him up.

The lowest order is the angels. And the plan has been revealed to it by God concerning every human being whom they watch over, because one angel from this lowest order accompanies every single human being in the world for his protection. And this is its service. The second order is the archangels. This is the service: directing everything in this creation according to the plan of God, whether powers or animals, birds, or creeping things, or fish, and to speak briefly and in short, whatever exists in this creation, besides human beings, they care for it and guide it. The third order, which is the archons. This is its service: moving the air so that a cloud rises from the ends of the earth, according to the words of David the prophet, and rain falls upon the earth. And this order makes all the variations in the atmosphere, sometimes rain and sometimes snow and sometimes hail and sometimes dust and sometimes blood. And it varies them. These also belong to this order: thunder and the fire of lightning.

This is its service: they keep the demons from destroying the creation of God out of their jealousy toward human beings; for if the cursed nature of the demons were allowed to accomplish the lust of its will, in an hour and moment they would overthrow the whole creation. But the divine power stops them, for a watch is set over them lest they succeed in achieving the lust of their will. The sixth order, which is the dominions. This is its service: they rule over kingdoms, and in their hands are victory and defeat in battle. And this is shown to be so by the example of the Assyrian king.

For when he went up against Jerusalem, an angel descended and ravaged the camp of the wicked, and one hundred eighty-five thousand died in one moment. And also the blessed Zechariah saw the angel in the form of a man riding on a red horse standing among the trees of the tabernacle, and following him were others on white and red horses with lances in their hands.

And Judah the Maccabee also saw the angel riding on a red horse all decked out with gold trappings. When they saw him, the camp of Antiochus the wicked fled before him. And wherever there is victory or defeat, these bestow it at the prompting of the living God, who commands them in the hour of battle.

The Testament of Abraham

On the day when I was destroying the gods of my father Terah and the gods of my brother Nahor, when I was testing which one was the truly strong god, at the time when my lot came up, when I had finished the services of my father Terah's sacrifice to his gods of wood, stone, gold, silver, brass and iron, I, Abraham, having entered their temple for the service, found a god named Mar-Umath, carved out of stone, fallen at the feet of an iron god, Nakhon. And it came to pass, that when I saw this, my heart was troubled. And I fell to thinking, because I, Abraham, was unable to return him to his place all by myself, since he was heavier than a great stone. And I went and told my father. And he entered with me. And as we both were moving him [Mar-Umath] to return him in his place, his head fell off of him, while I was still holding him by his head. And it came to pass, when my father saw that the head of Mar-Umath had fallen off of him, he said to me, "Abraham!" And I said, "Here am I!" And he said to me, "Bring me an axe and a chisel from the house." And I brought [them] to him from the house. And he carved another Mar-Umath, out of another stone, without a head, and [placed on him] the head that had been thrown down from Mar-Umath, and smashed the rest of Mar-Umath.

And he made five other gods, and he gave them to me [and] told me to sell them outside in the street of the town. And I saddled my father's ass and put them on it [and] went out to the main road to sell them. And behold, merchants from Paddan Aram came with camels to go to Egypt to buy kokonil from the Nile there. And I greeted them and they answered me. And I began to talk with them. One of their camels bellowed. The ass took fright and he ran and threw down the gods. And three of them were smashed and two remained. And it came to pass, when the Syrians saw that I had gods, they said to me, "Why did you not tell us that you had gods? We would have bought them before the ass heard the camel's cry and you would have had no loss. Give us at least the remaining gods and we will give you a proper price." And I thought [it over] in my heart. And they gave [also] the price of the smashed gods for the gods that remained. Since I had been distressed in my heart [wondering], "How would I let my father know about the matter?!" And the debris of the smashed [gods] I cast into the water of the river Gur, which was at that place. And they sank into the depths and were no more.

The Testament of Isaac

Now it came to pass, when the time had come for the Patriarch Isaac to go forth from the body, God sent to him the angel of his father Abraham at dawn on the twenty-second of Mesore. He said to him, "Hail, son of promise!" (Now it was the daily custom of the righteous old man Isaac to converse with the angels.) He lifted his face up to the face of the angel: he saw him assuming the likeness of his father Abraham; and he opened his mouth and raised his voice and cried out in great joy, "I have seen your face like someone who has seen the face of God." The angel said to him, "Listen, my beloved Isaac: I have been sent for you by God to take you to the heavens and set you beside your father Abraham, so that you can see all the saints; for your father is expecting you and is coming for you himself. Behold, a throne has been set up for you close to your father Abraham, and your lot and your beloved son Jacob's lot will surpass that of all others in the whole of God's creation that is why you have been given for evermore the name of Patriarch and Father of the World." But the God-loving old man Isaac said to the angel, "I am astonished by you, for you are my father". The angel answered, "My beloved Isaac, I am the angel that ministers to your father Abraham. But rejoice now, for I am to take you out of sorrow into gladness, out of suffering to rest for ever. I am to transport you from prison to a place where you can range at will — to a place of joy and gladness: I am to take you to where there is light and merriment and rejoicing and abundance that never fails. So then, draw up your testament and a statement for your household, for I am to translate you to rest for all eternity. Blessed is your father who begot you: blessed are you also: blessed is your son Jacob; and blessed are your descendants that will come after you."

Now Jacob heard them talking together, but he said nothing. Our father Isaac said to the angel with a heavy heart, "What shall I do about the light of my eyes, my beloved son Jacob? For I am afraid of what Esau might do to him - you know the situation." The angel said to him: "My beloved Isaac, if all the nations on earth were gathered together, they would not be able to bring these blessings pronounced over Jacob to nothing. When you blessed him, the Father and the Son and the Holy Spirit blessed him; and Michael and Gabriel and all the angels and all the heavenly ones and the spirits of all the righteous and your father Abraham all answered Amen. The sword therefore, shall not touch his body; but he shall be held in high honor and grow great and spread far and wide, and twelve thrones shall spring from him". Our father Isaac said to the angel: "You have given me much comfort, but do not let Jacob know in case he is distressed". The angel said to him: "My beloved Isaac, blessed is every righteous man who goes forth from the body: blessed are they when they meet with God.

Woe, woe, woe, three times woe to the sinner, because he has been born into this world: great sufferings will come to him.

Isaac, beloved of God, give these instructions, therefore, to your sons, and the instructions your father has given you. Hide nothing from Jacob, so that he can write them as instructions for the generations that will come after you, and those who love God may live their lives in accordance with them. And take care that I am able to fetch you with joy, without delay. The peace of my Lord that he has given me, I give to you, as I go to him who sent me".

The Testament of Jacob

Now it came to pass when the time had come for our beloved father Jacob the patriarch, the son of Isaac, the son of Abraham, to go forth from the body (and the God-loving Jacob was well on in years), the Lord sent Michael the archangel to him. And he said to him, "Israel, my beloved, you righteous root, write your words of instruction for your sons, and draw up your testament for them, and concern yourself about those of your household, for the time has come for you to go to your fathers and rejoice with them for ever." And when the God-loving Jacob heard this from the angel, he answered and said to him, "My lord - For it was his daily custom to talk to angels." He said to him, "May the will of the Lord be done."

God blessed our father Jacob. He made for himself a place apart, to which he withdrew and offered his prayers to God day and night, while the angels visited him and guarded him and kept him safe and gave him strength in everything. God blessed him; and his people increased greatly in numbers in the land of Egypt. For at the time he went down to Egypt to his son Joseph, his sight was failing as a result of continual weeping and worrying over his son Joseph; but after he arrived in Egypt and had seen his son Joseph's face, he saw everything clearly again. And Jacob Israel flung on his son Joseph's neck; he greeted him with tears and said: "Now let me die, for I have seen your face once more while you are still alive, my beloved". And Joseph ruled over the whole of Egypt. Jacob lived in the land of Goshen for seventeen years. He became very old and attained a great age: he kept all the commandments and lived always in the fear of the Lord: and his sight failed so that he could see no one because of extreme old age.

And when he had said this to him, the angel left him in peace and returned to the heavens, while Jacob gazed after him. And those who were in the house heard him giving thanks to the Lord and glorifying him with praises. And all his sons gathered round him, from the youngest to the eldest of them, all in tears and in great distress, saying, "He is about to go away and leave us." And they said to him. "What shall we do, beloved father, For we are aliens in a foreign land?" And Jacob said to them, "Do not be afraid, for God appeared to me in Mesopotamia saying: 'I am the God of your fathers: do not be afraid: I am with you for ever, and with your descendants that shall come after you for ever: the land on which you are standing I will give to you and your descendants for ever. And again he said to me, 'Do not be afraid to go down into Egypt; I will go with you down to Egypt; and I will increase your numbers, and your descendants shall flourish for ever, and Joseph shall lay his hands upon your eyes. And your people shall increase greatly in Egypt; and then they shall return to me here, and I will do them good because of you.' But now you must leave this place."

And after this the time drew near for Jacob Israel to go forth from the body. He called Joseph and spoke to him as follows: "If I have found favour with you, then put your blessed hand upon my thigh and swear to me on oath before the Lord to lay my body in my father's grave." And Joseph said to him, "I will do as you ask, my God-loving father." His father said to him, "I would have you swear" and Joseph swore the oath to Jacob his father that he would take his body to his father's grave. And Jacob bowed himself upon his son's neck.

Now after this it was reported to Joseph. Behold, your father is in a sorry state. He took his two sons, Ephraim and Manasseh and came to his father Israel. When Israel saw them, he said to Joseph, "Who are these, my son?" Joseph said to his father Jacob Israel: "These are my sons that God has given me in the land of my humiliation". Israel said: "Bring them near to me". Now Israel's sight had failed because of his great age, and he could hardly see. And Joseph brought them close to him; and he kissed them. When Israel had embraced them, he said, "God will add to your descendants". And Joseph made his two sons, Ephraim and Manasseh, do obeisance to him on the ground: Joseph put Manasseh under his right hand and Ephraim under his left hand. But Israel changed his hands: he laid his right hand on Ephraim's head and his left hand on Manasseh's head. And he blessed them; he gave them their patrimony, saying: "The God who approved my fathers Abraham and Isaac, The God who has looked after me from my childhood till today. The angel who rescues me from all my tribulations. Bless these lads who are my sons. With whom is left my name. And the name of my holy fathers Abraham and Isaac. They shall multiply; they shall increase; They shall become a great people on the earth." Afterwards Israel said to Joseph: "I am dying: but you will return to the land of your fathers, and God will be with you. Behold, you have been more favoured than your brothers, for I have taken the Amorites with my bow and my sword".

Jacob called all his sons and said to them, "Come to me. All of you, so that I can tell you what will happen to you. And also what will happen to each one of you at the end of time." All Israel's sons gathered round him, from the youngest to the eldest of them. Jacob Israel answered and said to his sons: "Listen, sons of Jacob, listen to Israel your father, from Reuben my first-born unto Benjamin". He told his sons what would happen to all twelve of them, name by name and tribe by tribe, with heaven's blessing. Then all kept silence so that he might rest a little.

He was taken up into the heavens to visit the resting-places. And behold, a host of tormentors came out.

The appearance of each one was different; and they were ready to torment the sinners - that is the fornicators, and the harlots, and the catamites, and the sodomites, and the adulterers, and those who have corrupted God's creation, and the magicians, and the sorcerers, and the unrighteous, and the idol-worshippers, and the astrologers, and the slanderers and the double-tongued. In short, many are the punishments for all the sins we have mentioned; the unquenchable fire, the outer darkness, the place where there shall be weeping and grinding of teeth, and the worm that does not sleep. And it is a terrible thing for you to be brought before the judge, and it is a terrible thing to come into the hands of the living God. Woe to all sinful men for whom these tortures and these tormentors are prepared. And again afterwards he took me and showed me the place where my fathers Abraham and Isaac were, a place that was all light; and they were glad and rejoiced in the kingdom of the heavens, in the city of the beloved. And he showed me all the resting-places and all the good things prepared for the righteous, and the things that eye has not seen nor ear heard, and have not come into the heart of men. that God has prepared for those who love him and do his will on earth (for if they end well, they do his will).

The Testament of Job

When we read that "there was a man in the land of Uz, whose name was Job," we are to understand a noble, conspicuous, influential, and altogether unique man. The narrator is not pointing to any man—a dramatic shadow, a figure which he intends to use for dramatic purposes; he is indicating the greatest man in the society to which that man belongs—say a typical man, the best specimen of humanity, altogether the finest, completest, strongest man. It is well to understand this because if there is to be any great contest between human nature and malign powers, we should like it to be as equal as possible. We should feel a sense of discontentment were the devil to challenge some puny creature—a man known only for his meanness and weakness.

On the other hand, we feel that the conditions are admirable as to their proportions and completeness, and the best, strongest, purest man is chosen to represent human nature in the tremendous contest. That is the case in the present instance.

The Testament of Moses

And it came to pass in the one hundred and twentieth year of the life of Moses, that is, the two thousand five hundredth year from the creation of the world, that he called to him Joshua the son of Nun, a man approved of the Lord, that he might be the minister of the people and of the tabernacle of the testimony with all its holy things, and that he might bring the people into the land given to their fathers, that it should be given to them according to the covenant and the oath, which he spoke in the tabernacle to give it by Joshua, saying to Joshua these words: "Be strong and of good courage according to thy might so as to do what has been commanded that thou mayst be blameless unto God." So saith the Lord of the world. For He hath created the world on behalf of His people. But He was not pleased to manifest this purpose of creation from the foundation of the world, in order that the Gentiles might thereby be convicted, yea to their own humiliation might by their arguments convict one another. Accordingly He designed and devised me, and He prepared me before the foundation of the world, that I should be the mediator of His covenant. And now I declare unto thee that the time of the years of my life is fulfilled and I am passing away to sleep with my fathers even in the presence of all the people. And receive thou this writing that thou mayst know how to preserve the books which I shall deliver unto thee: And thou shalt set these in order and anoint them with oil of cedar and put them away in earthen vessels in the place which He made from the beginning of the creation of the world, that His name should be called upon until the day of repentance in the visitation wherewith the Lord shall visit them in the consummation of the end of the days.

(And now) they will go by means of thee into the land which He determined and promised to give to their fathers, in the which thou shalt bless and give to them individually and confirm unto them their inheritance in me and establish for them the kingdom, and thou shalt appoint them prefectures according to the good pleasure of their Lord in judgment and righteousness. And (it will come to pass) in the sixth year after they enter into the land, that thereafter they shall be ruled by chiefs and kings for eighteen years, and during nineteen years the ten tribes will be apostates. And the twelve tribes will go down and transfer the tabernacle of the testimony. Then the God of heaven will make the court of His tabernacle and the tower of His sanctuary, and the two holy tribes will be (there) established: But the ten tribes will establish kingdoms for themselves according to their own ordinances. And they will offer sacrifices throughout twenty years: And seven will entrench the walls, and I will protect nine, but four will transgress the covenant of the Lord, and profane the oath which the Lord made with them.

And they will sacrifice their sons to strange gods, and they will set up idols in the sanctuary, to worship them. And in the house of the Lord they will work impiety and engrave every form of beast, even many abominations.

And in those days a king from the east will come against them and cover their land with his cavalry. And he will burn their colony with fire together with the holy temple of the Lord, and he will carry away all the holy vessels. And he will cast forth all the people, and he will take them to the land of his nativity, yea he will take the two tribes with him.

Then there will enter one who is over them, and he will spread forth his hands, and kneel upon his knees and pray on their behalf saying: "Lord of all, King on the lofty throne, who rulest the world, and didst will that this people should be Thine elect people, then (indeed) Thou didst will that Thou shouldst be called their God, according to the covenant which Thou didst make with their fathers. And yet they have gone in captivity into another land with their wives and their children, and around the gates of strange peoples and where there is great vanity. Regard and have compassion on them, O Lord of heaven." Then God will remember them on account of the covenant which He made with their fathers, and He will manifest His compassion in those times also. And He will put it into the mind of a king to have compassion on them, and he will send them off to their land and country. Then some portions of the tribes will go up and they will come to their appointed place, and they will entrench the place renewing it. And the two tribes will continue in their prescribed faith, sad and lamenting because they will not be able to offer sacrifices to the Lord of their fathers. And the ten tribes will increase and multiply among the Gentiles during the time of their captivity.

The Testament of Solomon

Testament of Solomon, son of David, who was king in Jerusalem, and mastered and controlled all spirits of the air, on the earth, and under the earth. By means of them also he wrought all the transcendent works of the Temple. Telling also of the authorities they wield against men, and by what angels these demons are brought to naught. Of the sage Solomon. Blessed art thou, O Lord God, who didst give Solomon such authority. Glory to thee and might unto the ages. Amen. And behold, when the Temple of the city of Jerusalem was being builded, and the artificers were working thereat, Ornias the demon came among them toward sunset; and he took away half of the pay of the chief-deviser's (?) little boy, as well as half his food.

He also continued to suck the thumb of his right hand every day. And the child grew thin, although he was very much loved by the king. So King Solomon called the boy one day, and questioned him, saying: "Do I not love thee more than all the artisans who are working in the Temple of God? Do I not give thee double wages and a double supply of food? How is it that day by day and hour by hour thow growest thinner?" But the child said to the king: "I pray thee, O king. Listen to what has befallen all that thy child hath. After we are all released from our work on the Temple of God, after sunset, when I lie down to rest, one of the evil demons comes and takes away from me one half of my pay and one half of my food. Then he also takes hold of my right hand and sucks my thumb. And lo, my soul is opressed, and so my body waxes thinner every day." Now when I Solomon heard this, I entered the Temple of God, and prayed with all my soul, night and day, that the demon might be delivered into my hands, and that I might gain authority over him.

And it came about through my prayer that grace was given to me from the Lord Sabaoth by Michael his archangel. [He brought me] a little ring, having a seal consisting of an engraved stone, and said to me: "Take, O Solomon, king, son of David, the gift which the Lord God has sent thee, the highest Sabaoth. With it thou shalt lock up all demons of the earth, male and female; and with their help thou shalt build up Jerusalem.

[But] thou [must] wear this seal of God. And this engraving of the seal of the ring sent thee is a Pentalpha." And I Solomon was overjoyed, and praised and glorified the God of heaven and earth.

And on the morrow I called the boy, and gave him the ring, and said to him: "take this, and at the hour in which the demon shall come unto thee, throw this ring at the chest of the demon, and say to him: 'In the name of God, King Solomon calls thee hither.' And then do thou come running to me, without having any misgivings or fear in respect of aught thou mayest hear on the part of the demon."

So the child took the ring, and went off; and behold, at the customary hour Ornias, the fierce demon, came like a burning fire to take the pay from the child. But the child according to the instructions received from the king, threw the ring at the chest of the demon, and said: "King Solomon calls thee hither." And then he went off at a run to the king. But the demon cried out aloud, saying: "Child, why hast thou done this to me?

I also appear as a lion, and I am commanded by all the demons. I am offspring of the archangel Uriel, the power of God." 1 Solomon, having heard the name of the archangel, prayed and glorified God, the Lord of heaven and earth. And I sealed the demon and set him to work at stone-cutting, so that he might cut the stones in the Temple, which, lying along the shore, had been brought by the Sea of Arabia. But he, fearful of the iron, continued and said to me: "I pray thee, King Solomon, let me go free; and I will bring you all the demons." And as he was not willing to be subject to me, I prayed the archangel Uriel to come and succour me; and I forthwith beheld the archangel Uriel coming down to me from the heavens. And the angel bade the whales of the sea come out of the abyss. And he cast his destiny upon the ground, and that [destiny] made subject [to him] the great demon. And he commanded the great demon and bold Ornias, to cut stones at the Temple. And accordingly I Solomon glorified the God of heaven and Maker of the earth. And he bade Ornias come with his destiny, and gave him the seal, saying: "Away with thee, and bring me hither the prince of all the demons." So Ornias took the finger-ring, and went off to Beelzeboul, who has kingship over the demons.

He said to him: "Hither! Solomon calls thee." But Beelzeboul, having heard, said to him: "Tell me, who is this Solomon of whom thou speakest to me?" Then Ornias threw the ring at the chest of Beelzeboul, saying: "Solomon the king calls thee." But Beelzeboul cried aloud with a mighty voice, and shot out a great burning flame of fire; and he arose, and followed Ornias, and came to Solomon. And when I saw the prince of demons, I glorified the Lord God, Maker of heaven and earth, and I said: "Blessed art thou, Lord God Almighty, who hast given to Solomon thy servant wisdom, the assessor of the wise, and hast subjected unto me all the power of the devil." And I questioned him, and said: "Who art thou?" The demon replied: "I am Beelzebub, the exarch of the demons. And all the demons have their chief seats close to me.

And I it is who make manifest the apparition of each demon." And he promised to bring to me in bonds all the unclean spirits. And I again glorified the God of heaven and earth, as I do always give thanks to him. I then asked of the demon if there were females among them. And when he told me that there were, I said that I desired to see them. So Beelzeboul went off at high speed, and brought unto me Onoskelis, that had a very pretty shape, and the skin of a fair-hued woman; and she tossed her head.

The Ascension of Isaiah

And it came to pass in the twenty-sixth year of the reign of Hezekiah king of Judah that he called Manasseh his son. Now he was his only one. And he called him into the presence of Isaiah the son of Amoz the prophet, and into the presence of Josab the son of Isaiah, in order to deliver unto him the words of righteousness which the king himself had seen, and of the eternal judgments and torments of Gehenna, and of the prince of this world, and of his angels, and his authorities and his powers. And the words of the faith of the Beloved which he himself had seen in the fifteenth year of his reign during his illness. And he delivered unto him the written words which Samnas the scribe had written, and also those which Isaiah, the son of Amoz, had given to him, and also to the prophets, that they might write and store up with him what he himself had seen in the king's house regarding the judgment of the angels, and the destruction of this world, and regarding the garments of the saints and their going forth, and regarding their transformation and the persecution and ascension of the Beloved.

The Beloved hath made of none effect thy design, and the purpose of thy heart will not be accomplished, for with this calling have I been called and I shall inherit the heritage of the Beloved. And Manasseh forsook the service of the God of his father, and he served Satan and his angels and his powers. And he turned aside the house of his father, which had been before the face of Hezekiah (from) the words of wisdom and from the service of God. And Manasseh turned aside his heart to serve Beliar; for the angel of lawlessness, who is the ruler of this world, is Beliar, whose name is Mantanbuchus.

And he delighted in Jerusalem because of Manasseh, and he made him strong in apostatizing (Israel) and in the lawlessness which were spread abroad in Jerusalem. And witchcraft and magic increased and divination and auguration, and fornication, [and adultery], and the persecution of the righteous by Manasseh and [Belachira, and] Tobia the Canaanite, and John of Anathoth, and by (Zadok) the chief of the works. And the rest of the acts, behold they are written in the book of the Kings of Judah and Israel. And, when Isaiah, the son of Amoz, saw the lawlessness which was being perpetrated in Jerusalem and the worship of Satan and his wantonness, he withdrew from Jerusalem and settled in Bethlehem of Judah. And these eat nothing save wild herbs which they gathered on the mountains, and having cooked them, they lived thereon together with Isaiah the prophet. And they spent two years of days on the mountains and hills.

And after this, whilst they were in the desert, there was a certain man in Samaria named Belchira, of the family of Zedekiah, the son of Chenaan, a false prophet, whose dwelling was in Bethlehem. Now Hezekiah the son of Chanani, who was the brother of his father, and in the days of Ahab, king of Israel, had been the teacher of the 400 prophets of Baal, had himself smitten and reproved Micaiah the son of Amada the prophet. And he, Micaiah, had been reproved by Ahab and cast into prison. (And he was) with Zedekiah the prophet: they were with Ahaziah the son of Ahab, king in Samaria. And Elijah the prophet of Tebon of Gilead was reproving Ahaziah and Samaria, and prophesied regarding Ahaziah that he should die on his bed of sickness, and that Samaria should be delivered into the hand of Leba Nasr because he had slain the prophets of God.

Joseph and Asenath

Pharaoh bestowed upon Joseph the name Zaphnath-paaneah due to his remarkable ability to interpret dreams, and he gave him Asenath, the daughter of Poti-pherah (also known as Pentephres), the priest of On (or Heliopolis), as his wife. Joseph then became a prominent figure throughout the land of Egypt. (Genesis 41:45)

Before the years of famine arrived, Asenath, the daughter of Poti-pherah, priest of On, bore Joseph two sons. (Genesis 41:50)

While residing in the land of Egypt, Joseph and Asenath, the daughter of Poti-pherah, priest of On, had two sons named Manasseh and Ephraim. (Genesis 46:20)

In the first year of the seven years of plenty, during the second month, Pharaoh dispatched Joseph to traverse the entirety of Egypt. Joseph arrived in the district of Heliopolis during the fourth month of the first year, specifically on the eighteenth day of the month. His mission involved gathering all the abundant harvest of the land, which was as plentiful as the sand of the sea.

Within the city of Heliopolis resided a man esteemed as a satrap of Pharaoh, holding the highest rank among Pharaoh's satraps and lords. This man, known as Pentephres, possessed great wealth, wisdom, and generosity. He served as Pharaoh's trusted counselor and held the esteemed position of priest of Heliopolis. Pentephres had a daughter, Aseneth, who was around eighteen years old, tall, and exceptionally beautiful, surpassing all other maidens in the land.

Aseneth stood out from the daughters of Egypt, resembling instead the daughters of the Hebrews. Her beauty became renowned throughout the land, captivating the hearts of many noble youths, including the sons of lords, satraps, and kings. Fierce competition arose among these suitors, leading to quarrels and disputes over Aseneth's affections.

Word of Aseneth's beauty even reached Pharaoh's eldest son, prompting him to request her hand in marriage from his father. He pleaded with Pharaoh, asking for Aseneth, the daughter of Pentephres, to be granted to him as his wife. However, Pharaoh questioned his son's desire for a bride of lower status, reminding him of his royal position and suggesting a union with a queenly bride instead, such as the daughter of King Joakim.

Life of Adam and Eve (Greek Apocalypse)

When Adam and Eve were expelled from paradise, they fashioned a tent for themselves and spent seven days mourning and lamenting in deep sorrow. After this time, hunger began to gnaw at them, and they sought food but found none. Eve, feeling the pangs of hunger, implored Adam to go in search of sustenance, hoping that God might show them mercy and restore them to their former abode.

Adam, stirred by Eve's plea, embarked on a journey across the land in search of food reminiscent of what they had in paradise. However, his quest proved futile, as he found only what animals consumed. Feeling despondent, Eve suggested that perhaps death would be preferable, as it might lead to their return to paradise, where they had erred and been banished. Yet, Adam reassured her, cautioning against such thoughts and urging them to seek a means of survival.

Their search continued for many days, but they found no sustenance comparable to the angelic food they had enjoyed in paradise. Adam reflected on the provisions the Lord had granted to animals and beasts, realizing that their plight called for repentance and penance. He proposed a great penitence, hoping that God would look upon them with compassion and provide for their needs.

Eve, eager to understand the nature of penitence, sought guidance from Adam, fearing that they might undertake a labor beyond their endurance. She expressed concern that their failure to fulfill their promises to God had caused Him to turn His face away from them. Adam, acknowledging Eve's limitations, advised her to perform as much penitence as she could, while he himself resolved to undertake forty days of fasting.

He instructed Eve to go to the Tigris River, take a stone, and stand in the water up to her neck, remaining silent to atone for their transgressions. Adam recognized the impurity of their lips, tainted by their disobedience to God's command regarding the forbidden tree.

Apocalypse of Moses

This is the story of Adam and Eve after their expulsion from Paradise. Adam knew his wife Eve, and they dwelled together to the east, under the sun, for eighteen years and two months. During this time, Eve conceived and bore two sons: Adiaphotos, called Cain, and Amilabes, called Abel.

One night, Eve dreamt that she saw Abel's blood being poured into Cain's mouth, and Cain drank it without mercy, ignoring Abel's pleas to spare him. Disturbed by this vision, Eve shared it with Adam, and they resolved to investigate its meaning, fearing that some harm had befallen their sons.

They discovered Abel murdered by the hand of Cain. God instructed the archangel Michael to tell Adam not to reveal what he knew to Cain, for Cain was a son of wrath. Yet, God promised to give Adam another son to guide him. Adam kept this secret, grieving for Abel.

In due time, Eve conceived and bore Seth, whom Adam recognized as a replacement for Abel. Adam and Eve gave thanks to God for their new son.

Adam lived for nine hundred and thirty years, during which he begat thirty sons and thirty daughters. As his time drew near, he called his children to him, expressing his suffering and longing for relief.

Seth proposed a remedy, suggesting that perhaps Adam yearned for the fruit of Paradise. Adam explained that his afflictions were not caused by longing for the fruit but by his disobedience to God's command not to eat from the forbidden tree.

Adam recounted how God had punished them for their disobedience, afflicting him with seventy-two strokes, each bringing its own suffering. Overwhelmed by his troubles, Adam lamented, and Eve offered to share his burden, blaming herself for their plight. Adam instructed Seth and Eve to go near Paradise, beseech God's mercy, and bring him oil from the tree of which the oil flowed. Meanwhile, Eve witnessed a beast attacking her son and lamented her role in their fall from grace.

The beast rebuked Eve, blaming her for their transformation and reminding her of her own disobedience. Eve realized the consequences of her actions and lamented the role she played in the downfall of humanity.

Apocalypse of Abraham

Once, a voice called out to me, speaking my name twice, "Abraham, Abraham!" and I responded, "Here am I!" The voice assured me, "Fear not, for I am before the worlds, a mighty God who hath created the light of the world. I am a shield over thee, thy helper." It instructed me to prepare a pure sacrifice of specific animals and to abstain from certain foods and drinks for forty days. Then, it promised to reveal the ages to come and show me great things because of my love for seeking out the divine.

Upon hearing this, I looked around but saw no one. My spirit trembled, and I fell to the ground like a stone, unable to stand. Then, a holy voice commanded Jaoel to strengthen me, and an angel appeared, grasping my hand and lifting me to my feet. He reassured me, calling me a friend of God and telling me not to fear, for he was sent to bless me.

I rose and beheld the angel, whose appearance was radiant and majestic. He encouraged me not to be afraid and invited me to accompany him to fulfill the sacrifice. We journeyed together for forty days and nights, during which I consumed no food or water but sustained myself by seeing and hearing the angel.

Finally, we arrived at the Mount of God, where I expressed my concern about the lack of a sacrifice or altar. The angel reassured me and instructed me to look around. To my amazement, all the sacrificial animals were following us. The angel directed me to slaughter and divide them, except for the birds, which he would take. He promised to show me wonders in heaven, on earth, and beyond, and I eagerly awaited the revelations to come.

Apocalypse of Adam

An ancient book known as the Apocalypse of Adam provides insights into mystical revelations and esoteric teachings. It is a part of the library known as Nag Hammadi, which was compiled in 1945 from early Christian Gnostic writings found in Egypt. Adam, the biblical character, is credited with writing this apocryphal work, which is presented as a revelation he received from God.

In the Apocalypse of Adam, Adam writes about his experiences and visions, offering light on creation mysteries, the nature of the divine, and the future of humanity. The book delves into several subjects, such as the origin of evil, the role of the archons, or material world gods, and the soul's journey.

A primary theme within the Apocalypse of Adam is the notion of gnosis, or spiritual wisdom. Adam is endowed by the divine realm with hidden wisdom that enables him to comprehend the true nature of existence and the divine plan. Adam reveals the mysteries of the universe and the divine hierarchy through his revelations.

The fall of humanity and the results of disobedience are also discussed in the text. It examines the account of Adam and Eve in the Garden of Eden, providing a complex analysis of their deeds and their spiritual implications. Predictions concerning the end of the world and the arrival of a savior who will free humanity from ignorance and injustice can be found in the Apocalypse of Adam. It describes a cosmic conflict between light and dark, with divine justice ultimately emerging victorious. The Apocalypse of Adam offers a distinctive viewpoint on biblical stories and spiritual teachings, as well as a fascinating look into early Christian Gnostic thought.

Apocalypse of Elijah

The word of Yahweh came to me saying, "Son of man, say to his people, 'why do you add sin to your sins and anger the Lord God who created you?' Don't love the world or the things which are in the world, for the boasting of the world and its destruction belong to the devil. Remember that the Lord of glory, Who created everything, had mercy upon you so that He might save us from the captivity of this age. For many times the devil desired not to let the sun rise above the earth and not to let the earth yield fruit, since he desires to consume men like a fire which rages in stubble, and he desires to swallow them like water. Therefore, on account of this, the God of glory had mercy upon us, and He sent His Son to the world so that He might save us from the captivity."

He did not inform an angel or an archangel or any principality when He was about to come to us, but He changed Himself to be like a man when He was about to come to us so that He might save use [from flesh]. Therefore become sons to Him since He is a father to you. Remember that He has prepared thrones and crowns for you in heaven, saying, "Everyone who will obey Me will receive thrones and crowns among those who are Mine." The Lord said, "I will write My name upon their forehead and I will seal their right hand, and they will not hunger or thirst. Neither will the son of lawlessness prevail over them, nor will the thrones hinder them, but they will walk with the angels up to My city." Now as for the sinners, they will be shamed and they will not pass by the thrones, but the thrones of death will seize them and rule over them because the angels will not agree with them.

They have alienated themselves from His dwellings. Hear, O wise men of the land, concerning the deceivers who will multiply in the last times so that they will set down for themselves doctrines which do not belong to God, setting aside the Law of God, those who have made their belly their God, saying, "The fast does not exist, nor did God create it," making themselves strangers to the covenant of God and robbing themselves of the glorious promises. Now these are not ever correctly established in the firm faith.

Therefore don't let those people lead you astray. Remember that from the time when He created the heavens, the Lord created the fast for a benefit to men on account of the passions and desires which fight against you so that the evil will not inflame you. "But it is a pure fast which I have created," said the Lord. The one who fasts continually will not sin although jealousy and strife are within him.

Let the pure one fast, but whenever the one who fasts is not pure he has angered the Lord and also the angels. And he has grieved his soul, gathering up wrath for himself for the day of wrath.

Furthermore, concerning the kings of Assyria and the dissolution of the heaven and the earth and the things beneath the earth. "Now therefore those who are Mine will not be overcome" says the Lord, "nor will they fear in the battle." When they see a king who rises in the north, who will be called "the king of Assyria" and "the king of injustice," he will increase his battles and his disturbances against Egypt. The land will groan together because your children will be seized. Many will desire death in those days, but death will flee from them. And a king who will be called "the king of peace" will rise up in the west. He will run upon the sea like a roaring lion. He will kill the king of injustice, and he will take vengeance on Egypt with battles and much bloodshed. It will come to pass in those days that he will command a peace and a vain gift in Egypt. He will give peace to these who are holy, saying, "The name of God is one." He will give honors to the saints and an exalting to the places of the saints. He will give vain gifts to the house of God. He will wander around in the cities of Egypt with guile, without their knowing. He will take count of the holy places. He will weigh the idols of the heathen. He will take count of their wealth. He will establish priests for them. He will command that the wise men and the great ones of the people be seized, and they will be brought to the metropolis which is by the sea, saying, "There is but one language." But when you hear, "Peace and joy exist," I will... Now I will tell you his signs so that you might know him. For he has two sons: one on his right and one on his left.

Apocalypse of Zephaniah

And a spirit took me and brought me up into the fifth heaven. And I saw angels who are called *lords*. And the diadem was set upon them in the Holy Spirit, and the throne of each of them was sevenfold more brilliant than the light of the rising sun. And they were dwelling in the temples of salvation and singing hymns to the ineffable God. I saw a soul which five thousand angels punished and guarded. They took it to the East and they brought it to the West. They beat its … they gave it a hundred … lashes for each one daily. I was afraid and I cast myself upon my face so that my joints dissolved. The angel helped me. He said unto me, "Be strong, O one who will triumph, and prevail so that thou wilt triumph over the accuser and thou wilt come up from Hades." And after I arose I said, "Who is this whom they are punishing?" He said unto me, "This is a soul which was found in its lawlessness." And before it attained to repenting it was visited, and taken out of its body. Truly, I, Zephaniah, saw these things in my vision. And the angel of the Lord went with me. I saw a great broad place, thousands of thousands surrounded it on its left side and myriads of myriads on its right side. The form of each one was different. Their hair was loose like that belonging to women. Their teeth were like the teeth of …dead. We will bury him like any man. Whenever he dies, we will carry him out playing the cithera before him and chanting psalms and odes over his body.

Now I went with the angel of the Lord, and he took me up over all my city. There was nothing before my eyes. Then I saw two men walking together on one road. I watched them as they talked. And, moreover, I also saw two women grinding together at a mill. And I watched them as they talked. And I also saw two upon a bed, each one of them acting for their mutual … upon a bed. And I saw the whole inhabited world hanging like a drop of water which is suspended from a bucket when it comes up from a well. I said unto the angel of the Lord, "Then does not darkness or night exist in this place?" He said unto me, "No, because darkness existeth not in that place where the righteous and the saints are, but rather they always exist in the light." And I saw all the souls of men as they existed in punishment. And I cried out to the Lord Almighty, "O God, if Thou remainest with the saints, Thou (certainly) hast compassion on behalf of the world and the souls which are in this punishment."

The angel of the Lord said unto me, "Come, let me show thee the place of righteousness." And he took me up upon Mount Seir and he showed me three men, as two angels walked with them rejoicing and exulting over them. I said to the angel, "Of what sort are these?"

He said to me, "These are the three sons of Joatham, the priest, who neither kept the commandment of their father nor observed the ordinances of the Lord."

Then I saw two other angels weeping over the three sons of Joatham, the priest. I said, "O angel, who are these?" He said, "These are the angels of the Lord Almighty. They write down all the good deeds of the righteous upon their scrolls as they watch at the gate of heaven." And I take them from their hands and bring them up before the Lord Almighty; He writeth their name in the Book of the Living. Also the angels of the accuser who is upon the earth, they also write down all the sins of men upon their scrolls. They also sit at the gate of heaven. They tell the accuser and he writeth them upon his scroll so that he might accuse them when they come out of the world and go down there.

Apocalypse of Sedrach

And he [Sedrach] heard a hidden voice in his ears: "Here, Sedrach, you who wish and desire to talk with God and to ask him to reveal to you the things that you wish to ask." And Sedrach said, "What is it, my Lord?" And the voice said to him, "I was sent to you that I may carry you up into heaven." And he said, "I want to speak to God face to face, but I am not able, Lord, to ascend into the heavens." But the angel, having stretched out his wings, took him and went up into the heavens, and took him up as far as the third heaven, and the flame of the divinity stood there.

And the Lord said to him, "Welcome, my dear Sedrach. What kind of complaint do you have against the God who created you, for you have said, 'I want to speak with God face to face'?" Sedrach said to him, "Indeed, the son does have a complaint against the Father: My Lord, what did you create the earth for?" The Lord said to him, "For man." Sedrach said, "What did you create the sea for and why did you spread every good thing upon the earth?" The Lord said, "For man." Sedrach said to him, "If you have done these things, why did you destroy man?" And the Lord said, "Man is my work and the creature of my hands, and I discipline him as I find it right." Sedrach said to him, "Your discipline is punishment and fire; and they are very bitter, my Lord. It would be better for man if he were not born. Indeed, what have you done, my Lord; for what reason did you labor with your spotless hands and create man, since you did not desire to have mercy upon him?" God said to him, "I created the first man, Adam, and placed him in Paradise in the midst of which is the tree of life, and I said to him, 'Eat of all the fruit, only beware of the tree of life, for if you eat from it you will surely die.' However, he disobeyed my commandment and having been deceived by the devil he ate from the tree."

Apocalypse of Lamech

When Methuselah comes to ask Enoch about the Watchers' fate, Enoch tells Methuselah about how the fallen Watchers bemoaned their terrible circumstances and how hopeless their future appeared to be. They had begged Enoch to record their prayer to Yehuweh for mercy. He speaks with Methuselah and elaborates on the fate of the fallen Watchers, explaining why they have not been pardoned for their sins, after fully informing Methuselah of the contents of the Watchers' petition.

Methuselah reports to Lamech the words of Enoch; Lamech marries Batenos and has passionate sex with her. She conceives and gives birth to a son of glorious and angelic appearance. Lamech is extremely afraid and believes that his wife had sex with an angel. He is very angry with his wife, but his wife promises that she has not slept with any other being than Lamech. Lamech, still not convinced, goes to his father, Methuselah, for help. Methuselah goes to Enoch to learn the truth about the father of Batenos son. Methuselah finds his father Enoch and explains to him why he has come to him. Enoch prophesies of the destruction of the world by a flood because of the sins resulting from the corruption of creation by the Watchers. He prophesies of a chosen one intended by Yeuweh to preserve a remnant. He prophesies about the future history related to the coming of the chosen one.

Enoch concludes his prophetic discourse by ensuring Methuselah that Lamech is truly the father of Noah, and that he should send this message to Lamech, and that he should inform him about the great things, that his son should be named Noah, and that he is the one chosen through whom Yeuweh will restore peace and purity to the earth. Methuselah informs his son Lamech about his son Noah, and Lamech rejoices that he is truly the father of Noah.

Apocalypse of Ezra

In the thirtieth year of the fall of our city, I, Salathiel, who am Ezra, was in Babylon, and lay stretched upon my bed and was troubled, and thoughts were coming up upon my heart, because I saw the desolation of Sion and the wealth of the dwellings of Babylon; and my spirit was sore amazed, and I began to speak to the Most High words of fear. And it gave thee Adam, a dead body, and he was the formation of thy hands; and thou didst breathe in him the breath of life and he was living before thee; and thou leddest him into Paradise which thy right hand did plant before ever the earth came.

And to this one thou didst give the commandment, and he transgressed it; and forthwith thou didst decree upon him death, and upon his generations. And from him were born peoples and tribes and tongues and clans which are without number. And all peoples followed their (own) works, and dealt wickedly and were ungodly before thee— and thou didst not hinder them. But again in due time thou didst bring the Flood upon the earth and upon the inhabitants of the world, and thou didst destroy them; and their destruction was alike, and as to Adam (came) death, so to them (came) the death of the Flood.

Nevertheless thou didst spare one of them with his household—and from him all the righteous are descended. And it came to pass when the inhabitants of the earth began to multiply, and multiplied children and peoples and many multitudes, and began again to be ungodly more than the former generations—it came to pass that when they practiced ungodliness before thee, thou didst choose one of them for thyself, whose name was Abraham; and thou didst love him, and thou didst show him the consummation of the times, him alone, between thee and him by night; and thou didst establish with him an everlasting covenant, and didst promise him that thou wouldest never forsake his seed.

And thou gavest him Isaac, and to Isaac thou gavest Jacob and Esau; and thou didst choose thee Jacob for an heritage, and Esau thou didst hate; and Jacob became a great people. And when thou didst bring up his seed from Egypt [and didst establish with him an everlasting covenant], and didst bring them to Mount Sinai, Thou didst incline the heavens, and didst shake the earth and madest the world to quake, and causedst the deeps to tremble, and didst alarm the worlds. And the infirmity remained in them, and (also) the Law, together with the evil root; then what was good departed, and the evil came. And the times passed away, and the seasons were ended; and thou didst raise up for thyself a servant whose name was David; and thou commandedst him to build a city for thy name [and a House] that oblations from thine own might be offered therein.

And this was done many years. But the inhabitants of the city sinned against thee and did nothing new beyond what Adam had done and all his generations; for they also were clothing themselves with the evil heart. And (so) thou deliveredst thy City into the hand of thine enemies. And then I said in my heart: Are then the inhabitants of Babylon behaving well? And hast thou for this forsaken Sion? And it came to pass when I came hither I saw many ungodlinesses which cannot be numbered, and many iniquities my soul saw this thirty years; and my heart was perturbed, because I have seen how thou dost suffer the sinners, and sparest the ungodly, and hast destroyed thy people, and preserved thine enemies; and hast not made known unto any how thy way may be comprehended.

Hath Babylon behaved better than Sion? Or knowest thou any other people more than Israel? Or what tribe hath believed thy covenant as Jacob hath—they whose reward is not seen, and whose labour hath not borne fruit! For I have gone about through the peoples and have seen that they are now prosperous although unmindful of thy commandments. But now weigh thou in the balance our iniquities and those of the inhabitants of the world, and the poise of the scale will be seen to be not inclined. Or when have the inhabitants of the world not sinned before thee? Or what people hath so kept thy commandments? Men, however, with names thou mayest find who have kept thy commandments, but a people thou shalt not find.

Apocalypse of Baruch

And it came to pass in the twenty-fifth year of Jeconiah king of Judah, that the word of the Lord came to Baruch the son of Neriah, and said to him: "Hast thou seen all that this people are doing to Me, that the evils which these two tribes which remained have done are greater than those of the ten tribes which were carried away captive? For the former tribes were forced by their kings to commit sin, but these two of themselves have been forcing and compelling their kings to commit sin. For this reason, behold I bring evil upon this city, and upon its inhabitants, and it will be removed from before Me for a time. And do ye, heavens, withhold your dew, and open not the treasuries of rain. And do thou, sun, withhold the light of thy rays; and do thou, moon, extinguish the multitude of thy light; for why should light rise again where the light of Zion is darkened? And you, ye bridegrooms, enter not in, and let not the brides adorn themselves with garlands; and, ye women, pray not that ye may bear. For the barren shall rejoice more, and those who have no sons shall be glad, and those who have sons shall have anguish. For why should they bear in pain and bury in grief? Or wherefore, again, should mankind have sons; or wherefore should the seed of their nature again be named, where that mother is desolate, and her sons are led into captivity? From this time forward speak not of beauty and discourse not of gracefulness. Moreover, ye priests, take ye the keys of the sanctuary and cast them into the height of heaven, and give them to the Lord, and say: Guard Thy house Thyself, for lo! we are found false stewards. And you, ye virgins, who spin fine linen and silk with gold of Ophir, hasten and take all things and cast them into the fire, that it may bear them to Him who made them, and the flame send them to Him who created them, lest the enemy get possession of them." Moreover, I, Baruch, say this against thee, Babylon: "If thou hadst prospered, and Zion had dwelt in her glory, it would have been a great grief to us that thou shouldst be equal to Zion. But now, lo! the grief is infinite, and the lamentation measureless, for lo! thou art prospered and Zion desolate. Who will be judge regarding these things? Or to whom shall we complain regarding that which has befallen us? Lord, how hast Thou borne it? Our fathers went to rest without grief, and lo! the righteous sleep in the earth in tranquillity."

Apocalypse of Peter

On the first day of the week, a multitude gathered together, and they brought many sick people to Peter, that he might cure them. And one of the multitude was bold enough to say unto Peter, "Peter, behold, before our eyes thou didst make many blind see and deaf hear and the lame walk, and hast helped the weak, and given them strength; why hast thou not helped thy Virgin daughter, which grew up beautifully and believed on the name of God? For behold, one of her sides is wholly paralyzed, and there she is helpless in the corner. One can see those which thou hast cured; but for thy own daughter thou didst not care."

But Peter smiled and said to him, "My son, God alone knows why her body is sick. Know that God is not unable or powerless, to give his present to my daughter. But that thy soul may be convinced and those present believe the more," he looked at his daughter and said to her, "Arise from thy place with the help of none except Jesus alone, and walk wholly before those present and come to me." And she arose and came to him. The multitude rejoiced over that which had taken place. And Peter said to them, "Behold, your hearts are convinced that God is not powerless concerning the things which we ask of him." They rejoiced the more and glorified God. Said Peter to his daughter, "Return to thy place, sit down there, and be helpless again, for it is good for me and thee." And the girl did as she was bidden, and became as before. The whole multitude wept and besought Peter to make her whole.

When Paul was at Rome and confirmed many in the faith, it also happened that a certain woman named Candida, wife of Quartus the custodian, heard Paul and listened to his words and became a believer. And when she on her part had instructed her husband, who became a believer, Quartus persuaded Paul to leave the city (and to go) wherever he pleased. Paul said to him, "If such be the will of God, he will reveal it to me." And Paul fasted three days and besought the Lord to grant what were good for him, and in a vision he saw the Lord, who said to him, "Paul, arise, and in thy body be a physician to the Spaniards!" At this he related to the brethren what God had commanded (him), and without hesitation he made ready to leave the city.

Apocalypse of Paul

As Paul was going up to Iconium after his flight from Antioch, his fellow-travelers were Demas and Hermogenes, the coppersmith, full of hypocrisy, and persisted in staying with Paul, as if they loved him. Paul looking only to the goodness of Christ, did them no harm, but loved them exceedingly, so that he made sweet to them all the words of the Lord and the oracles of the gospel concerning the birth and resurrection of the Beloved; and he gave them an account, word for word, of the great deeds of Christ, how they were revealed to him [that Christ is born of the virgin Mary and of the seed of David].

And a certain man, by name Onesiphorus, hearing that Paul was to come to Iconium, went out to meet him with his children Simmias and Zeno, and his wife Lectra, in order that he might entertain him. For Titus had informed him what Paul was like in appearance. For he had not seen him in the flesh, but only in the spirit.

And he went along the royal road to Lystra, and kept looking at the passers-by according to the description of Titus. And he saw Paul coming, a man small in size, bald-headed, bandy-legged, of noble mien, with eyebrows meeting, rather long-nosed, full of grace. For sometimes he seemed like a man, and sometimes he had the countenance of an angel.

Apocalypse of Thomas

Here beginneth the epistle of the Lord unto Thomas.

Hear thou, Thomas, the things which must come to pass in the last times: there shall be famine and war and earthquakes in divers places, snow and ice and great drought shall there be and many dissensions among the peoples, blasphemy, iniquity, envy and villainy, indolence, pride and intemperance, so that every man shall speak that which pleaseth him.

And my priests shall not have peace among themselves, but shall sacrifice unto me with deceitful mind: therefore will I not look upon them. Then shall the priests behold the people departing from the house of the Lord and turning unto the world and setting up landmarks in the house of God. And they shall claim vindicate for themselves many things and places that were lost and that shall be subject unto Caesar as also they were aforetime: giving poll-taxes of for the cities, even gold and silver and the chief men of the cities shall be condemned and their substance brought into the treasury of the kings, and they shall be filled.

For there shall be great disturbance throughout all the people, and death. The house of the Lord shall be desolate, and their altars shall be abhorred, so that spiders weave their webs therein. The place of holiness shall be corrupted, the priesthood polluted, distress agony shall increase, virtue shall be overcome, joy perish, and gladness depart. In those days evil shall abound: there shall be respecters of persons, hymns shall cease out of the house of the Lord, truth shall be no more, covetousness shall abound among the priests; an upright man shall not be found.

On a sudden there shall arise near the last time a king, a lover of the law, who shall hold rule not for long: he shall leave two sons. The first is named of the first letter (A, Arcadius), the second of the eighth (H, Honorius). The first shall die before the second.

Thereafter shall arise two princes to oppress the nations under whose hands there shall be a very great famine in the right-hand part of the east, so that nation shall rise up against nation and be driven out from their own borders.

Again another king shall arise, a crafty man, and shall command a golden image of Caesar to be made wherefore martyrdoms shall abound. Then shall faith return unto the servants of the Lord, and holiness shall be multiplied and distress agony increase.

The mountains shall the comforted and shall drop down sweetness of fire from the facet, that the number of the saints may be accomplished.

After a little space there shall arise a king out of the east, a lover of the law, who shall cause all good things and necessary to abound in the house of the Lord: he shall show mercy unto the widows and to the needy, and command a royal gift to be given unto the priests: in his days shall be abundance of all things.

And after that again a king shall arise in the south part of the world, and shall hold rule a little space: in whose days the treasury shall fail because of the wages of the Roman soldiers so that the substance of all the aged shall be commanded to be taken and given to the king to distribute.

Thereafter shall be plenty of corn and wine and oil, but great dearness of money, so that the substance of gold and silver shall be given for corn, and there shall be great dearth.

At that time shall be very great rising of the sea, so that no man shall tell news to any man. The kings of the earth and the princes and the captains shall be troubled, and no man shall speak freely boldly. Grey hairs shall be seen upon boys, and the young shall not give place unto the aged.

After that shall arise another king, a crafty man, who shall hold rule for a short space: in whose days there shall be all manner of evils, even the death of the race of men from the east even unto Babylon. And thereafter death and famine and sword in the land of Chanaan even unto Rome. Then shall all the fountains of waters and wells boil over and be turned into blood. The heaven shall be moved, the stars shall fall upon the earth, the sun shall be cut in half like the moon, and the moon shall not give her light. There shall be great signs and wonders in those days when Antichrist draweth near.

Apocalypse of Stephen

Two years after the Ascension there was a contest about Jesus. Many learned men had assembled at Jerusalem from Ethiopia, the Thebaid, Alexandria, Jerusalem, Asia, Mauretania and Babylon. There was a great clamour among them like thunder, lasting till the fourth hour.

Stephen, a learned man of the tribe of Benjamin, stood on a high place and addressed the assembly. "Why this tumult?" said he. Blessed is he who has not doubted concerning Jesus. Born of a pure virgin he filled the world with light. By Satan's contrivances Herod slew 14,000 (144,000) children. He spoke of the miracles of Jesus. Woe to the unbelievers when he shall come as judge, with angels, a fiery chariot, a mighty wind: the stars shall fall, the heavens open, the books be brought forward. The twelve angels who are set over every soul shall unveil the deeds of men. The sea shall move and give up what is in it. The mountains fall, all the surface of the earth becomes smooth. Great winged thrones are set. The Lord, and Christ, and the Holy Spirit take their seats. The Father bids Jesus sit on his right hand.

At this point the crowd cried out: "Blasphemy!" and took Stephen before Pilate.

They led Stephen away. Caiaphas ordered him to be beaten till the blood ran. And he prayed: Lay not this sin to their charge. We saw how angels ministered to him.

In the morning Pilate called his wife and two children: they baptized themselves and praised God.

Stephen lifted up his hands and said: "Silence, persecutor! Recognize the Son of God. Thou makest me doubt of my own descent. But I see that thou shalt ere long drink of the same cup as I. What thou doest, do quickly." Saul rent his clothes and beat Stephen. Gamaliel, Saul's teacher, sprang forth and gave Saul a buffet, saying: "Did I teach thee such conduct? Know that what this man saith is acceptable and good."

Saul was yet more enraged, and looked fiercely on him, saying: "I spare thine old age, but thou shalt reap a due reward for this." Gamaliel answered: "I ask nothing better than to suffer with Christ." The elders rent their clothes, cast dust on their heads, and cried: "Crucify the blasphemers!"

Saul said: "Guard them until the morrow." Next day he sat on the judgement seat and had them brought before him, and they were led away to be crucified. An angel came and cast away the cross, and Stephen's wounds were healed. Seven men came and poured molten lead into his mouth and pitch into his ears. They drove nails into his breast and feet, and he prayed for their forgiveness. Again an angel came down and healed him, and a great multitude believed.

The Gospel of the Hebrews

Hebrews is about the supremacy of Christ Jesus. It paints a wonderful picture of how He is superior to the angels because of His redemptive work on the cross. Jesus is the exact representation of the Father and was sent to communicate to us the true nature of God. By understanding who Jesus is and what He said, we can know the fullness of God's nature and character.

Jesus was briefly humbled and took on human form so he could taste death for everyone. It was fitting that Jesus, through whom everything exists, was the author of salvation. He shared in humanity so that through His death he might destroy him who holds the power of death. We must pay close attention to this so we do not ignore such a great salvation.

It shows His superiority to Moses and the covenant of the law. This chapter also serves as a warning against hardness of heart and being lured away by sin and unbelief. We are to encourage each other daily and stand strong until the end with confidence in Christ.

This rest for God's people is what was promised throughout the entire Old Testament. True Sabbath rest does not come from adhering to the law or taking a break from work one day of the week. The believer's rest comes to fulfillment in our lives by fellowshipping with Christ. Hebrews further shows Jesus as God's appointed High priest who became the source of eternal salvation for everyone who believes. He was subjected to the weakness of the flesh yet without sin. He learned obedience through what he suffered so in the same way he is able to help those who will inherit salvation. Jesus was designed by God to be our high priest forever in the order of Melchizedek.

The Gospel of the Ebionites

And they (the Ebionites) receive the Gospel according to Matthew. For this they too, like the followers of Cerinthus and Merinthus, use to the exclusion of others. And they call it according to the Hebrews, as the truth is, that Matthew alone of New Testament writers made his exposition and preaching of the Gospel in Hebrew and in Hebrew letters.

Epiphanius goes on to say that he had heard of Hebrew versions of *John* and *Acts* kept privately in the treasuries (Geniza?) at Tiberias, and continues:

In the Gospel they have, called according to Matthew, but not wholly complete, but falsified and mutilated (they call it the Hebrew *Gospel*), it is contained what follows:

There was a certain man named Jesus, and he was about thirty years old, who chose us. And coming unto Capernaum he entered into the house of Simon who was surnamed Peter, and opened his mouth and said: "As I passed by the lake of Tiberias, I chose John and James the sons of Zebedee, and Simon and Andrew and (Philip and Bartholomew, James the son of Alphaeus and Thomas) Thaddaeus and Simon the Zealot and Judas the Iscariot: and thee, Matthew, as thou satest as the receipt of custom I called, and thou followedst me. You therefore I will to be twelve apostles for a testimony unto (of) Israel." And:

John was baptizing, and there went out unto him Pharisees and were baptized, and all Jerusalem. And John had raiment of camel's hair and a leathern girdle about his loins: and his meat (it saith) was wild honey, whereof the taste is the taste of *manna*, as a cake dipped in oil. That, forsooth, they may pervert the word of truth into a lie and for locusts put a cake dipped in honey (*sic*).

And the beginning of their Gospel says that: It came to pass in the days of Herod the king of Judaea (when Caiaphas was high priest) that there came (a certain man) John (by name), baptizing with the baptism of repentance in the river Jordan, who was said to be of the lineage of Aaron the priest, child of Zecharias and Elisabeth, and all went out unto him.

The borrowing from St. Luke is very evident here. He goes on.

And after a good deal more it continues that:

After the people were baptized, Jesus also came and was baptized by John; and as he came up from the water, the heavens were opened, and he saw the Holy Ghost in the likeness of a dove that descended and entered into him: and a voice from heaven saying: Thou art my beloved Son, in thee I am well pleased: and again: This day have I begotten thee. And straightway there shone about the place a great light. Which when John saw (it saith) he saith unto him: "Who art thou, Lord?" and again there was a voice from heaven saying unto him: "This is my beloved Son in whom I am well pleased." And then (it saith) John fell down before him and said: "I beseech thee, Lord, baptize thou me." But he prevented him saying: "Suffer it (or let it go): for thus it behoveth that all things should be fulfilled."

The Gospel of the Nazarenes

The Book of the Generation of Jesus, the Son of David, the Son of Abraham:

Abraham begat Isaac; and Isaac begat Jacob; and Jacob begat Judas and his brethren. And Judas begat Phares and Zara of Thamar; and Phares begat Esrom; and Esrom begat Aram. And Aram begat Aminadab; and Aminadab begat Naasson; and Naasson begat Salmon. And Salmon begat Booz of Rachab; and Booz begat Obed of Ruth; and Obed begat Jesse. And Jesse begat David the king; and David the king begat Solomon of her that had been the wife of Urias. And Solomon begat Roboam; and Roboam begat Abia; and Abia begat Asa. And Asa begat Josaphat; and Josaphat begat Joram; and Joram begat Ozias. And Ozias begat Joatham; and Joatham begat Achaz; and Achaz begat Ezekias. And Ezekias begat Manasses; and Manasses begat Amon; and Amon begat Josias; And Josias begat Jechonias and his brethren, about the time they were carried away to Babylon. And after they were brought to Babylon, Jechonias begat Salathiel; and Salathiel begat Zorobabel. And Zorobabel begat Abiud; and Abiud begat Eliakim; and Eliakim begat Abner; and Abner begat Azor. And Azor begat Sadoc; and Sadoc begat Achim; and Achim begat Eliud. And Eliud begat Eleazar; and Eleazar begat Matthan; and Matthan begat Jacob. And Jacob begat Joseph the husband of Mary, of whom was born Jesus, who is called Christ.

So all the generations from Abraham to David are fourteen generations; and from David until the carrying away into Babylon are fourteen generations; and from the carrying away into Babylon unto Christ are fourteen generations.

Now the birth of Jesus was on this wise: When as his mother Mary was espoused to Joseph, before they came together, she was found with child of the Holy Ghost. Then Joseph her husband, being a just man, and not willing to make her a public example, was minded to deliver her up privately. But while he thought on these things, behold, the angel of the Lord appeared unto him in a dream, saying, Joseph, thou son of David, fear not to take unto thee Mary thy wife: for that which is conceived in her is of the Holy Ghost. And she shall bring forth a son, and thou shalt call his name Jesus: for he shall save my people from their sins.

Now all this was done, that it might be fulfilled which was spoken of the Lord through Isaiah his prophet, saying, Behold, a virgin shall be with child, and shall bring forth a son, and they shall call his name Emmanuel, which being interpreted is, God with us.

Then Joseph being raised from sleep did as the angel of the Lord had bidden him, and took unto him his wife: And knew her not till she had brought forth her firstborn son: and he called his name Jesus.

Now when Jesus was born in Bethlehem of Judaea in the days of Herod the king, behold, there came wise men from the east to Jerusalem, Saying, "Where is he that is born King of the Jews? For we have seen his star in the east, and are come to worship him." When Herod the king had heard these things, he was troubled, and all Jerusalem with him. And when he had gathered all the chief priests and scribes of the people together, he demanded of them where Christ should be born. And they said unto him, "In Bethlehem of Judaea: for thus it is written by the prophet, 'And thou Bethlehem, in the land of Juda, art not the least among the princes of Juda: for out of thee shall come a Governor, that shall rule my people Israel.'"

Then Herod, when he had privately called the wise men, enquired of them diligently what time the star appeared. And he sent them to Bethlehem, and said, "Go and search diligently for the young child; and when ye have found him, bring me word again, that I may come and worship him also." When they had heard the king, they departed; and, lo, the star, which they saw in the east, went before them, till it came and stood over where the young child was. When they saw the star, they rejoiced with exceeding great joy. And when they were come into the house, they saw the young child with Mary his mother, and fell down, and worshipped him: and when they had opened their treasures, they presented unto him gifts; gold, and frankincense and myrrh.

And being warned by the angel of God in a dream that they should not return to Herod, they departed into their own country another way.

The Gospel of the Egyptians

The holy book of the Egyptians about the great invisible Spirit, the Father whose name cannot be uttered, he who came forth from the heights of the perfection, the light of the light of the aeons of light, the light of the silence of the providence (and) the Father of the silence, the light of the word and the truth, the light of the incorruptions, the infinite light, the radiance from the aeons of light of the unrevealable, unmarked, ageless, unproclaimable Father, the aeon of the aeons, Autogenes, selfbegotten, self-producing, alien, the really true aeon.

In contrast with more ancient history where it was simply assumed that each tribe had its gods (ancestors); now, one becomes concerned with the *true* God. This god is called the Autogenes; being self-begotten (the *really true aeon*), but is also said to be the Anthropos, that besides being the archetypal human, is also the savior figure (Seth). Three powers came forth from him; they are the Father, the Mother, (and) the Son, from the living silence, what came forth from the incorruptible Father. These came forth from the silence of the unknown Father. And from that place, Domedon Doxomedon came forth, the aeon of the aeons and the light of each one of their powers. And thus the Son came forth fourth; the Mother fifth; the Father sixth. He was but unheralded; it is he who is unmarked among all the powers, the glories, and the incorruptions.

From that place, the three powers came forth, the three ogdoads that the Father brings forth in silence with his providence, from his bosom, i.e., the Father, the Mother, and the Son. The first ogdoad, because of which the thrice-male child came forth, which is the thought, and the word, and the incorruption, and the eternal life, the will, the mind, and the foreknowledge, the androgynous Father. The second ogdoad-power, the Mother, the virginal Barbelon, who presides over the heaven, the uninterpretable power, the ineffable Mother. She originated from herself; she came forth; she agreed with the Father of the silent silence.

The third ogdoad-power, the Son of the silent silence, and the crown of the silent silence, and the glory of the Father, and the virtue of the Mother, he brings forth from the bosom the seven powers of the great light of the seven voices. And the word is their completion. These are the three powers, the three ogdoads that the Father, through his providence, brought forth from his bosom. He brought them forth at that place. Domedon Doxomedon came forth, the aeon of the aeons, and the throne which is in him, and the powers which surround him, the glories and the incorruptions. The

Father of the great light who came forth from the silence, he is the great Doxomedon-aeon, in which the thrice-male child rests.

And the throne of his glory was established in it, this one on which his unrevealable name is inscribed, on the tablet one is the word, the Father of the light of everything, he who came forth from the silence, while he rests in the silence, he whose name is in an invisible symbol.

The Gospel of Mary

In the Gospel of Mary, there are parallels to traditions and sayings found in texts that later formed part of the New Testament. Some of these parallels involve significant words or phrases, while others relate to broader thematic similarities or even contrasts with the New Testament. The precise status of these parallels is subject to dispute. Here, the discussion primarily focuses on whether the similarities and parallels in wording indicate any kind of dependence of the Gospel of Mary on New Testament texts, and if so, whether we can pinpoint the sources of the language used in the Gospel of Mary.

It's important to note that the Gospel of Mary never explicitly *quotes* any text. The author of the Gospel of Mary doesn't use introductory formulas such as "as it is written," as Paul does at times to introduce quotations from Jewish scripture. Instead, the parallels noted in the Gospel of Mary remain at the level of possible allusions. If we define *quotation* or *citation* as instances where a writer explicitly signals the intention to repeat words found in an earlier text, then there are no such quotations in the Gospel of Mary, whether from Jewish scripture or from texts that later became part of the Christian scripture in the New Testament. Rather, there are at most possible allusions to various sayings that appear in texts later considered canonical for Christians. Notably, there are several possible allusions to texts from the later canonical gospels, as well as some potential echoes of Pauline passages.

The parallels between the Gospel of Mary and New Testament texts can be categorized into three groups:

(1) Clear echoes or allusions to New Testament passages;
(2) Parallels that are less direct and not clearly echoes of New Testament passages;
(3) More general thematic parallels.

Such a division is inherently subjective, as what may seem like a clear echo or allusion to one modern scholar might be less evident to another. Overall, the aim of this discussion is to analyze the relationship between the Gospel of Mary and New Testament texts, considering the context and purpose of the Gospel of Mary's composition.

The Gospel of Philip

Christ came to ransom some, to save others, to redeem others. He ransomed those who were strangers and made them his own. And he set his own apart, those whom he gave as a pledge according to his plan. It was not only when he appeared that he voluntarily laid down his life, but he voluntarily laid down his life from the very day the world came into being. Then he came first in order to take it, since it had been given as a pledge. It fell into the hands of robbers and was taken captive, but he saved it. He redeemed the good people in the world as well as the evil. Light and Darkness, life and death, right and left, are brothers of one another. They are inseparable. Because of this neither are the good good, nor evil evil, nor is life life, nor death death. For this reason each one will dissolve into its earliest origin. But those who are exalted above the world are indissoluble, eternal.

Names given to the worldly are very deceptive, for they divert our thoughts from what is correct to what is incorrect. Thus one who hears the word "God" does not perceive what is correct, but perceives what is incorrect. So also with "the Father" and "the Son" and "the Holy Spirit" and "life" and "light" and "resurrection" and "the Church (Ekklesia)" and all the rest - people do not perceive what is correct but they perceive what is incorrect, unless they have come to know what is correct. The names which are heard are in the world deceive. If they were in the Aeon (eternal realm), they would at no time be used as names in the world. Nor were they set among worldly things. They have an end in the Aeon. One single name is not uttered in the world, the name which the Father gave to the Son; it is the name above all things: the name of the Father. For the Son would not become Father unless he wore the name of the Father. Those who have this name know it, but they do not speak it. But those who do not have it do not know it.

But truth brought names into existence in the world for our sakes, because it is not possible to learn it (truth) without these names. Truth is one single thing; it is many things and for our sakes to teach about this one thing in love through many things. The rulers (archons) wanted to deceive man, since they saw that he had a kinship with those that are truly good.

These things they knew, for they wanted to take the free man and make him a slave to them forever. These are powers which man, not wishing him to be saved, in order that they may. For if man is saved, there will not be any sacrifices and animals will not be offered to the powers.

Indeed, the animals were the ones to whom they sacrificed. They were indeed offering them up alive, but when they offered them up, they died. As for man, they offered him up to God dead, and he lived.

Before Christ came, there was no bread in the world, just as Paradise, the place were Adam was, had many trees to nourish the animals but no wheat to sustain man. Man used to feed like the animals, but when Christ came, the perfect man, he brought bread from heaven in order that man might be nourished with the food of man. The rulers thought that it was by their own power and will that they were doing what they did, but the Holy Spirit in secret was accomplishing everything through them as it wished. Truth, which existed since the beginning, is sown everywhere. And many see it being sown, but few are they who see it being reaped.

The Gospel of Truth

The Gospel of Truth is a Christian sermon focusing on the theme of salvation through acquaintance with God (gnosis). It stands as one of the most finely crafted works of ancient Christian literature, likely possessing a rhetorical power comparable to the great masterpieces of Christian prose in its original Greek form. Serving as the earliest surviving sermon of Christian mysticism, it offers a rare glimpse into the human atmosphere of a church meeting within the ancient gnostic sect and its offshoots, where a magisterial gnostic preacher addresses a congregation with personal authority. The opening sentence establishes the main themes of the work: the quest for the Father (God) and the hope of deliverance for those who have fallen into ignorance, requiring a savior to ransom them from their lack of understanding. It speaks of the emission of the saving divine Word, who reveals the truth about the Father and brings joy and acquaintance with Him. Thus, the contents of the Gospel of Truth dynamically describe Christian gnosis, or acquaintance with God.

The theological drama within the text revolves around three characters: the Father (the unknowable God), the Word or Son (God's manifestation), and the ignorant who are transformed into those with acquaintance. Although overtly Christian, the work does not explicitly reference the gnostic myth. It emphasizes Jesus' crucifixion as the central object of Christian faith and contains numerous paraphrases of New Testament passages. The proclamation of truth brings joy to those who have received grace from the Father of Truth, enabling them to learn about Him through the power of the Word emanating from His fullness. This Word, referred to as the Savior, accomplishes the work of ransoming those who are ignorant of the Father. The term "proclamation" signifies the manifestation of hope for those seeking Him.

Acquaintance with the Father and the appearance of His Son provide a means for comprehension. When individuals see, hear, taste, smell, and touch the Son, they gain insight into the Father and His will. Many who receive this light turn to Him, having been strangers to His image and previously unrecognized by Him. The text also discusses the concept of "Matter," from which the Son comes in a fleshly likeness without hindrance. This incorruptibility signifies unseizability, speaking in new terms about what is in the Father's heart. The Word, free from defect, produces light and gives birth to life, imparting thought, intelligence, mercy, salvation, and the powerful spirit from the Father's infinity and sweetness. Through the Son, punishments and torments cease, as He unchains and reproves those who have strayed from mercy, guiding them into acquaintance with God.

The Gospel of the Twelve

There was in the days of Herod, the king of Judea, a certain priest named Zacharias, of the course of Abia; and his wife was of the daughters of Aaron, and her name was Elisabeth. And they were both righteous before God, walking in all the commandments and ordinances of the Lord blameless. They had no child, because Elisabeth was barren, and they were both well stricken in years. And it came to pass, while Zacharias executed the priest's office before God in the order of his course, according to the custom of the priest's office, his lot was to burn incense when he went into the temple of the Lord. And the whole multitude of the people were praying without at the time of the offering of incense. An angel of the Lord appeared unto him, standing over the altar of incense. When Zacharias saw him, he was troubled, and fear fell upon him. But the angel said unto him, "Fear not, Zacharias, for thy prayer is heard; and thy wife Elisabeth shall bear thee a son, and thou shalt call his name John. And thou shalt have joy and gladness; and many shall rejoice at his birth; for he shall be great in the sight of the Lord, and shall neither eat flesh meats, nor drink strong drink; and he shall be filled with the Holy Spirit, even from his mother's womb. He shall turn many of the children of Israel to the Lord their God. And he shall go before Him in the spirit and power of Elias, to turn the hearts of the fathers to the children, and the disobedient to the wisdom of the just; to make ready a people prepared for the Lord."

Zacharias said unto the angel, "Whereby shall I know this? For I am an old man, and my wife is well stricken in years." The angel, answering, said unto him, "I am Gabriel, that stand in the presence of God; and am sent to speak unto thee, and to announce unto thee these glad tidings. And, behold, thou art dumb, and not able to speak, until the day that these things shall be performed, then shall thy tongue be loosed that thou mayest believe my words which shall be fulfilled in their season." The people waited for Zacharias, and marveled that he tarried so long in the temple. When he came out, he could not speak unto them; and they perceived that he had seen a vision in the temple; for he made signs unto them, and remained speechless. And it came to pass, as soon as the days of his ministration were accomplished, he departed to his own house. After those days, Elisabeth conceived, and hid herself five months, saying, "Thus hath the Lord dealt with me in the days wherein he looked on me, to take away my reproach among men."

In the sixth month, the angel Gabriel was sent from God unto a city of Galilee, named Nazareth, to a virgin espoused to a man named Joseph, of the house of David; and the virgin's name was Mary. Now Joseph was a just and rational Mind, skilled in all manner of work in wood and stone.

Mary was a tender and discerning Soul, and she wrought veils for the temple. They were both pure before God; and of them both was Jesu-Maria, who is called the Christ. The angel came in unto Mary and said, "Hail, Mary, thou that art highly favored, for the Motherhood of God is with thee: blessed art thou among women and blessed be the fruit of thy womb." When she saw him, she was troubled at his saying, and cast in her mind what manner of salutation this should be. The angel said unto her, "Fear not, Mary, for thou hast found favor with God and, behold, thou shalt conceive in thy womb and bring forth a child, and He shall be great and shalt be called a Son of the Highest. The Lord God shall give unto him the throne of his father David: and he shall reign over the house of Jacob for ever; and of his kingdom there shall be no end." Mary said unto the angel, "How shall this be, seeing I know not a man?" The angel answered and said unto her, "The Holy Spirit shall come upon Joseph thy Spouse, and the power of the Highest shall overshadow thee, O Mary; therefore also that holy thing which shall be born of thee shall be called the Christ, the Child of God, and his Name on earth shall be called Jesu-Maria, for he shall save the people from their sins, whosoever shall repent and obey his Law.

Therefore ye shall eat no flesh, nor drink strong drink, for the child shall be consecrated unto God from its mother's womb, and neither flesh nor strong drink shall he take, nor shall razor touch his head. And, behold, thy cousin Elisabeth, she hath also conceived a son in her old age: and this is the sixth month with her, who was called barren. For with God no thing shall be impossible." Mary said, "Behold the handmaid of the Lord; be it unto me according to thy word." The angel departed from her. In the same day, the angel Gabriel appeared unto Joseph in a dream and said unto him, "Hail, Joseph, thou that art highly favored, for the Fatherhood of God is with thee. Blessed art thou among men and blessed be the fruit of thy loins."

And the devil said unto Hades: "Why affrightest thou me, Hades? It is a prophet, and he hath made himself like unto God: this prophet will we take and bring him hither unto those that think to ascend into heaven." And Hades said: "Which of the prophets is it? Show me: Is it Enoch the scribe of righteousness? But God hath not suffered him to come down upon the earth before the end of the six thousand years. Sayest thou that it is Elias, the avenger? But before he cometh not down. What shall I do, whereas the destruction is of God: for surely our end is at hand? For I have the number (of the years) in mine hands."

The Gospel of Bartholomew

After the resurrection from the dead of our Lord Jesus Christ, Bartholomew came unto the Lord and questioned him, saying: Lord, reveal unto me the mysteries of the heavens. Jesus answered and said unto him: "If I put off the body of the flesh, I shall not be able to tell them unto thee." But when he was buried and risen again, they all durst not question him, because it was not to look upon him, but the fullness of his Godhead was seen. Bartholomew therefore drew near unto the Lord and said: "I have a word to speak unto thee, Lord." And Jesus said to him: "I know what thou art about to say; say then what thou wilt, and I will answer thee."

Bartholomew said: "Lord, when thou wentest to be hanged upon the cross, I followed thee afar off and saw thee hung upon the cross, and the angels coming down from heaven and worshipping thee. And when there came darkness, I beheld, and I saw thee that thou wast vanished away from the cross and I heard only a voice in the parts under the earth, and great wailing and gnashing of teeth on a sudden. Tell me, Lord, whither wentest thou from the cross?" Jesus answered and said: "Blessed art thou, Bartholomew, my beloved, because thou sawest this mystery, and now will I tell thee all things whatsoever thou askest me. For when I vanished away from the cross, then went I down into Hades that I might bring up Adam and all them that were with him, according to the supplication of Michael the archangel."

Then said Bartholomew: "Lord, what was the voice which was heard?" Jesus saith unto him: "Hades said unto Beliar: As I perceive, a God cometh hither. And the angels cried unto the powers, saying: Remove your gates, ye princes, remove the everlasting doors, for behold the King of glory cometh down." Hades said: "Who is the King of glory, that cometh down from heaven unto us?" And when I had descended five hundred steps, Hades was troubled, saying: "I hear the breathing of the Most High, and I cannot endure it. He cometh with great fragrance and I cannot bear it." But the devil answered and said: "Submit not thyself, O Hades, but be strong: for God himself hath not descended upon the earth."

But when I had descended yet five hundred steps, the angels and the powers cried out: "Take hold, remove the doors, for behold the King of glory cometh down!" And Hades said: "O, woe unto me, for I hear the breath of God!" And Beliar said unto Hades: "Look carefully who it is that , for it is Elias, or Enoch, or one of the prophets that this man seemeth to me to be." But Hades answered Death and said: "Not yet are six thousand years accomplished. And whence are these, O Beliar; for the sum of the number is in mine hands.

Be not troubled, make safe thy gates and strengthen thy bars: consider, God cometh not down upon the earth. Hades saith unto him: "These be no good words that I hear from thee: my belly is rent, and mine inward parts are pained: it cannot be but that God cometh hither. Alas, whither shall I flee before the face of the power of the great king? Suffer me to enter into myself (thyself): for before thee was I formed." Bartholomew saith unto him: "I saw thee again, hanging upon the cross, and all the dead arising and worshipping thee, and going up again into their sepulchres.

Tell me, Lord, who was he whom the angels bare up in their hands, even that man that was very great of stature?" Jesus answered and said unto him: "It was Adam the first-formed, for whose sake I came down from heaven upon earth." And I said unto him: "I was hung upon the cross for thee and for thy children's sake." And he, when he heard it, groaned and said: "So was thy good pleasure, O Lord." Again Bartholomew said: "Lord, I saw the angels ascending before Adam and singing praises. But one of the angels which was very great, above the rest, would not ascend up with them: and there was in his hand a sword of fire, and he was looking steadfastly upon thee only." And Jesus said unto him: "Blessed art thou, Bartholomew my beloved because thou sawest these mysteries.

This was one of the angels of vengeance which stand before my Father's throne: and this angel sent he unto me. And for this cause he would not ascend up, because he desired to destroy all the powers of the world. But when I commanded him to ascend up, there went a flame out of his hand and rent asunder the veil of the temple, and parted it in two pieces for a witness unto the children of Israel for my passion because they crucified me."

The Gospel of Nicodemus (Acts of Pilate)

Christ was accused to Pilate by the Jews of healing on the Sabbath. Summoned before Pilate by a messenger who does him honour. Worshipped by the standards bowing down to him. Annas and Caiphas, and Summas, and Datam, Gamaliel, Judas, Levi, Nepthalim, Alexander, Cyrus, and other Jews, went to Pilate about Jesus, accusing him with many bad crimes.

And said, "We are assured that Jesus is the son of Joseph, the carpenter, and born of Mary, and that he declares himself the Son of God, and a king; and not only so, but attempts the dissolution of the Sabbath, and the laws of our fathers." Pilate replied, "What is it which he declares? And what is it which he attempts dissolving?" The Jews told him, "We have a law which forbids doing cures on the Sabbath day; but he cures both the lame and the deaf, those afflicted with the palsy, the blind, the lepers, and demoniacs, on that day, by wicked methods." Pilate replied, "How can he do this by wicked methods?" They answered: "He is a conjurer, and casts out devils by the prince of the devils; and so all things become subject to him." Then said Pilate, "Casting out devils seems not to be the work of an unclean spirit, but to proceed from the power of God."

The Jews replied to Pilate, "We entreat your highness to summon him to appear before your tribunal, and hear him yourself." Then Pilate called a messenger, and said to him, "By what means will Christ be brought hither?" Then went the messenger forth, and knowing Christ, worshipped him; and having spread the cloak which he had in his hand upon the ground, he said, "Lord, walk upon this, and go in, for the governor calls thee. "When the Jews perceived what the messenger had done, they exclaimed against him to Pilate, and said, "Why did you not give him his summons by a beadle, and not by a messenger?" — For the messenger, when he saw him, worshipped him, and spread the cloak which he had in his hand upon the ground before him, and said to him, Lord, the governor calls thee.

Then Pilate called the messenger, and said, "Why hast thou done thus?" The messenger replied, "When thou sentest me from Jerusalem to Alexander, I saw Jesus sitting in a mean figure upon a she-ass", and the children of the Hebrews cried out, "Hosannah, holding boughs of trees in their hands. Others spread their garments in the way, and said, Save us, thou who art in heaven; blessed is he who cometh in the name of the Lord."

The Gospel of the Lord (by Marcion)

In the fifteenth year of the reign of Tiberius Caesar, Pontius Pilatus being the Governor of Judaea, Jesus came down to Capernaum, a city in Galilee, and was teaching on the sabbath days: and they were astonished at his doctrine: for his word was in authority. And in the synagogue there was a man who had a spirit of an unclean demon, and he cried out with a loud voice, Saying, "Let us alone; what have we to do with thee, Jesus? Art thou come to destroy us? I know thee who thou art: the Holy One of God." And Jesus rebuked him, saying; "Hold thy peace, and come out of him." And when the demon had thrown him into the midst, he came out of him, having done no hurt. And amazement came upon all, and they spoke together saying to one another, "What is this word?" For in authority and power he commandeth the unclean spirits, and they come out. And a rumour of him went out into every place of the country round about. And he arose out of the synagogue, and entered into the house of Simon. And Simons mother in law was taken with a great fever: and they besought him for her. And he stood over her, and rebuked the fever: and it left her: and immediately she arose and ministered unto them. And he came to Nazareth, and went into the synagogue on the Sabbath day and sat down. And the eyes of all in the synagogue fastened on him. And he began to speak to them; and all wondered at the words which proceedeth from his mouth. And he said unto them, " Ye will surely say unto me this parable, Physician, heal thyself; whatsoever we have heard done at Capernaum, do also here. But I tell you of a truth, many widows were in Israel in the days of Elijah, when the heaven was shut up three years and six months, when great famine occurred throughout all the land: and unto none of them was Elijah sent, but only to Sarepta, a city of Sidon, unto a woman that was a widow. And many lepers were in Israel in the time of Elisha the prophet: and none of them was cleansed, but only Naaman the Syrian". And they were all filled with wrath in the synagogue, when they heard these things, and rose up, and thrust him out of the city, and led him unto the brow of the hill whereon their city was built, to cast him down headlong.

But he passing through the midst of them went his way. And when the sun was setting, all as many as had any sick with divers diseases brought them unto him; and he laid his hands on every one of them, and healed them. And demons also came out of many, crying out, saying, "Thou art Son of God" and he rebuked them suffered them not to speak; for they knew that he was the Christ. And when it was day, he departed and went into a desert place: and the multitudes sought him, and came unto him, and stayed him, that he should not depart from them.

And he said unto them, "I must announce as good tidings the kingdom of God to the other cities also: for therefore am I sent." And he was preaching in the synagogues of Galilee.

And it came to pass in those days, that he went out into the mountains to pray, and was passing the whole night in prayer to God. And when it was day, he called unto him his disciples: and he chose from them twelve, whom he also named apostles; Simon (whom was also named Peter), and Andrew his brother, James and John, Philip and Bartholomew, Matthew and Thomas, James the son of Alphaeus, and Simon whom they called Zelotes, and Judas the brother of James, and Judas Iscariot, which also became a traitor. And he came down among them, and stood on a level place, and the multitude of his disciples, and a great number of people out of all Judaea and Jerusalem, and from the sea coast of Tyre and Sidon, which came to hear him, and to be healed of their diseases; and they that were troubled by unclean spirits: and they were healed. And the whole multitude sought to touch him: for power went out of him, and healed them all. And he lifted up his eyes on his disciples, and said: "Blessed are ye poor: for yours is the kingdom of God. Blessed are ye that hunger now: for ye shall be filled. Blessed are ye that weep now: for ye shall laugh.

Blessed are ye, when men shall hate you, and when they shall separate you from their company, and shall reproach you, and cast out your name as evil, for the Son of man's sake. Rejoice ye in that day, and leap for you: for, behold, your reward is great in heaven: for according to these things did their fathers unto the prophets. But woe unto you that are rich! For ye have consolation in full. Woe unto you that are full! For ye shall hunger. Woe unto you that laugh now! For ye shall mourn and weep. Woe unto you, when all men shall speak well of you! For according to these things did their fathers to the false prophets. But I say unto you that hear, Love your enemies, do good to them which hate you, bless them that curse you, and pray for them which despitefully use you. Unto him that smiteth thee on the one cheek, offer also the other; and from him that taketh away thy cloke, withhold not thy coat also. Give every man that asketh of thee: and of him that taketh away thy goods ask them."

Pseudo-Matthew

Here beginneth the book of the Birth of the Blessed Mary and the Infancy of the Saviour. Written in Hebrew by the Blessed Evangelist Matthew, and translated into Latin by the Blessed Presbyter Jerome. To their well–beloved brother Jerome the Presbyter, Bishops Cromatius and Heliodorus in the Lord, greeting. The birth of the Virgin Mary, and the nativity and infancy of our Lord Jesus Christ, we find in apocryphal books. But considering that in them many things contrary to our faith are written, we have believed that they ought all to be rejected, lest perchance we should transfer the joy of Christ to Antichrist. While, therefore, we were considering these things, there came holy men, Parmenius and Varinus, who said that your Holiness had found a Hebrew volume, written by the hand of the most blessed Evangelist Matthew, in which also the birth of the virgin mother herself, and the infancy of our Saviour, were written. And accordingly we entreat your affection by our Lord Jesus Christ Himself, to render it from the Hebrew into Latin, not so much for the attainment of those things which are the insignia of Christ, as for the exclusion of the craft of heretics, who, in order to teach bad doctrine, have mingled their own lies with the excellent nativity of Christ, that by the sweetness of life they might hide the bitterness of death. It will therefore become your purest piety, either to listen to us as your brethren entreating, or to let us have as bishops exacting, the debt of affection which you may deem due.

In those days there was a man in Jerusalem, Joachim by name, of the tribe of Judah. He was the shepherd of his own sheep, fearing the Lord in integrity and singleness of heart. He had no other care than that of his herds, from the produce of which he supplied with food all that feared God, offering double gifts in the fear of God to all who laboured in doctrine, and who ministered unto Him. Therefore his lambs, and his sheep, and his wool, and all things whatsoever he possessed, he used to divide into three portions: one he gave to the orphans, the widows, the strangers, and the poor; the second to those that worshipped God; and the third he kept for himself and all his house. And as he did so, the Lord multiplied to him his herds, so that there was no man like him in the people of Israel. This now he began to do when he was fifteen years old. And at the age of twenty he took to wife Anna, the daughter of Achar, of his own tribe, that is, of the tribe of Judah, of the family of David. And though they had lived together for twenty years, he had by her neither sons nor daughters.

And it happened that, in the time of the feast, among those who were offering incense to the Lord, Joachim stood getting ready his gifts in the sight of the Lord. And the priest, Ruben by name, coming to him, said: It is not lawful for thee to stand among those who are doing sacrifice to God, because God has not blessed thee so as to give thee seed in Israel. Being therefore put to shame in the sight of the people, he retired from the temple of the Lord weeping, and did not return to his house, but went to his flocks, taking with him his shepherds into the mountains to a far country, so that for five months his wife Anna could hear no tidings of him. And she prayed with tears, saying: "O Lord, most mighty God of Israel, why hast Thou, seeing that already Thou hast not given me children, taken from me my husband also? Behold, now five months that I have not seen my husband; and I know not where he is tarrying; nor, if I knew him to be dead, could I bury him." And while she wept excessively, she entered into the court of His house; and she fell on her face in prayer, and poured out her supplications before the Lord. At the same time there appeared a young man on the mountains to Joachim while he was feeding his flocks, and said to him: "Why dost thou not return to thy wife?" And Joachim said: "I have had her for twenty years, and it has not been the will of God to give me children by her. I have been driven with shame and reproach from the temple of the Lord: why should I go back to her, when I have been once cast off and utterly despised? Here then will I remain with my sheep; and so long as in this life God is willing to grant me light, I shall willingly, by the hands of my servants, bestow their portions upon the poor, and the orphans, and those that fear God."

After these things, her nine months being fulfilled, Anna brought forth a daughter, and called her Mary. And having weaned her in her third year, Joachim, and Anna his wife, went together to the temple of the Lord to offer sacrifices to God, and placed the infant, Mary by name, in the community of virgins, in which the virgins remained day and night praising God. And when she was put down before the doors of the temple, she went up the fifteen steps so swiftly, that she did not look back at all; nor did she, as children are wont to do, seek for her parents. Whereupon her parents, each of them anxiously seeking for the child, were both alike astonished, until they found her in the temple, and the priests of the temple themselves wondered. Then Anna, filled with the Holy Spirit, said before them all: "The Lord Almighty, the God of Hosts, being mindful of His word, hath visited His people with a good and holy visitation, to bring down the hearts of the Gentiles who were rising against us, and turn them to Himself. He hath opened His ears to our prayers: He hath kept away from us the exulting of all our enemies. The barren hath become a mother, and hath brought forth exultation and gladness to Israel. Behold the gifts which I have brought to offer to my Lord, and mine enemies have not been able to hinder me. For God hath turned their hearts to me, and Himself hath given me everlasting joy."

The Infancy Gospel of Thomas

The stories of Thomas the Israelite, the Philosopher, concerning the works of the Childhood of the Lord.

I, Thomas the Israelite, tell unto you, even all the brethren that are of the Gentiles, to make known unto you the works of the childhood of our Lord Jesus Christ and his mighty deeds, even all that he did when he was born in our land: whereof the beginning is thus:

This little child Jesus when he was five years old was playing at the ford of a brook: and he gathered together the waters that flowed there into pools, and made them straightway clean, and commanded them by his word alone. And having made soft clay, he fashioned thereof twelve sparrows. And it was the Sabbath when he did these things (or made them). And there were also many other little children playing with him.

And a certain Jew when he saw what Jesus did, playing upon the Sabbath day, departed straightway and told his father Joseph: Lo, thy child is at the brook, and he hath taken clay and fashioned twelve little birds, and hath polluted the Sabbath day. And Joseph came to the place and saw: and cried out to him, saying: "Wherefore doest thou these things on the Sabbath, which it is not lawful to do?" But Jesus clapped his hands together and cried out to the sparrows and said to them: "Go!" and the sparrows took their flight and went away chirping. And when the Jews saw it they were amazed, and departed and told their chief men that which they had seen Jesus do.

But the son of Annas the scribe was standing there with Joseph; and he took a branch of a willow and dispersed the waters which Jesus had gathered together. And when Jesus saw what was done, he was wroth and said unto him: "O evil, ungodly, and foolish one, what hurt did the pools and the waters do thee? Behold, now also thou shalt be withered like a tree, and shalt not bear leaves, neither root, nor fruit." And straightway that lad withered up wholly, but Jesus departed and went unto Joseph's house. But the parents of him that was withered took him up, bewailing his youth, and brought him to Joseph, and accused him 'For that thou hast such a child which doeth such deeds.'

After that again he went through the village, and a child ran and dashed against his shoulder. And Jesus was provoked and said unto him: "Thou shalt not finish thy course (lit. go all thy way)."

And immediately he fell down and died. But certain when they saw what was done said: "Whence was this young child born, for that every word of his is an accomplished work?"

And the parents of him that was dead came unto Joseph, and blamed him, saying: "Thou that hast such a child canst not dwell with us in the village: or do thou teach him to bless and not to curse: for he slayeth our children."

And Joseph called the young child apart and admonished him, saying: "Wherefore doest thou such things, that these suffer and hate us and persecute us?" But Jesus said: "I know that these thy words are not thine: nevertheless for thy sake I will hold my peace: but they shall bear their punishment." And straightway they that accused him were smitten with blindness. And they that saw it were sore afraid and perplexed, and said concerning him that every word which he spake whether it were good or bad, was a deed, and became a marvel. And when they (he?) saw that Jesus had so done, Joseph arose and took hold upon his ear and wrung it sore. And the young child was wroth and said unto him: "It sufficeth thee (or them) to seek and not to find, and verily thou hast done unwisely: knowest thou not that I am thine? Vex me not."

Now a certain teacher, Zacchaeus by name, stood there and he heard in part when Jesus said these things to his father and he marvelled greatly that being a young child he spake such matters. And after a few days he came near unto Joseph and said unto him: "Thou hast a wise child, and he hath understanding. Come, deliver him to me that he may learn letters. And I will teach him with the letters all knowledge and that he salute all the elders and honour them as grandfathers and fathers, and love them of his own years." And he told him all the letters from Alpha even to Omega clearly, with much questioning. But Jesus looked upon Zacchaeus the teacher and saith unto him: "Thou that knowest not the Alpha according to its nature, how canst thou teach others the Beta? Thou hypocrite, first, if thou knowest it, teach the Alpha, and then will we believe thee concerning the Beta." Then began he to confound the mouth of the teacher concerning the first letter, and he could not prevail to answer him. And in the hearing of many the young child saith to Zacchaeus: "Hear, O teacher, the ordinance of the first letter and pay heed to this, how that it hath [what follows is really unintelligible in this and in all the parallel texts: a literal version would run something like this: how that it hath lines, and a middle mark, which thou seest, common to both, going apart; coming together, raised up on high, dancing (a corrupt word), of three signs, like in kind (a corrupt word), balanced, equal in measure]: thou hast the rules of the Alpha."

The Arabic Infancy Gospel

In the name of the Father, and the Son, and the Holy Spirit, one God.

With the help and favour of the Most High we begin to write a book of the miracles of our Lord and Master and Saviour Jesus Christ, which is called the Gospel of the Infancy: in the peace of the Lord. Amen.

We find what follows in the book of Joseph the high priest, who lived in the time of Christ. Some say that he is Caiaphas. He has said that Jesus spoke, and, indeed, when He was lying in His cradle said to Mary His mother: "I am Jesus, the Son of God, the Logos, whom thou hast brought forth, as the Angel Gabriel announced to thee; and my Father has sent me for the salvation of the world."

In the three hundred and ninth year of the era of Alexander, Augustus put forth an edict, that every man should be enrolled in his native place. Joseph therefore arose, and taking Mary his spouse, went away to Jerusalem, and came to Bethlehem, to be enrolled along with his family in his native city. And having come to a cave, Mary told Joseph that the time of the birth was at hand, and that she could not go into the city; but, said she, let us go into this cave. This took place at sunset. And Joseph went out in haste to go for a woman to be near her. When, therefore, he was busy about that, he saw an Hebrew old woman belonging to Jerusalem, and said: "Come hither, my good woman, and go into this cave, in which there is a woman near her time."

Wherefore, after sunset, the old woman, and Joseph with her, came to the cave, and they both went in. And, behold, it was filled with lights more beautiful than the gleaming of lamps and candles, and more splendid than the light of the sun. The child, enwrapped in swaddling clothes, was sucking the breast of the Lady Mary His mother, being placed in a stall. And when both were wondering at this light, the old woman asks the Lady Mary: "Art thou the mother of this Child?" And when the Lady Mary gave her assent, she says: "Thou art not at all like the daughters of Eve." The Lady Mary said: "As my son has no equal among children, so his mother has no equal among women." The old woman replied: "My mistress, I came to get payment; I have been for a long time affected with palsy." Our mistress the Lady Mary said to her: "Place thy hands upon the child." And the old woman did so, and was immediately cured. Then she went forth, saying: "Henceforth I will be the attendant and servant of this child all the days of my life."

Then came shepherds; and when they had lighted a fire, and were rejoicing greatly, there appeared to them the hosts of heaven praising and celebrating God Most High. And while the shepherds were doing the same, the cave was at that time made like a temple of the upper world, since both heavenly and earthly voices glorified and magnified God on account of the birth of the Lord Christ. And when that old Hebrew woman saw the manifestation of those miracles, she thanked God, saying: "I give Thee thanks, O God, the God of Israel, because mine eyes have seen the birth of the Saviour of the world."

And the time of circumcision, that is, the eighth day, being at hand, the child was to be circumcised according to the law. Wherefore they circumcised Him in the cave. And the old Hebrew woman took the piece of skin; but some say that she took the navel-string, and laid it past in a jar of old oil of nard. And she had a son, a dealer in unguents, and she gave it to him, saying: "See that thou do not sell this jar of unguent of nard, even although three hundred denarii should be offered thee for it." And this is that jar which Mary the sinner bought and poured upon the head and feet of our Lord Jesus Christ, which thereafter she wiped with the hair of her head. Ten days after, they took Him to Jerusalem; and on the fortieth day after His birth they carried Him into the temple, and set Him before the Lord, and offered sacrifices for Him, according to the command-meet of the law of Moses, which is: "Every male that openeth the womb shall be called the holy of God."

Then old Simeon saw Him shining like a pillar of light, when the Lady Mary, His virgin mother, rejoicing over Him, was carrying Him in her arms. And angels, praising Him, stood round Him in a circle, like life guards standing by a king. Simeon therefore went up in haste to the Lady Mary, and, with hands stretched out before her, said to the Lord Christ: "Now, O my Lord, let Thy servant depart in peace, according to Thy word; for mine eyes have seen Thy compassion, which Thou hast prepared for the salvation of all peoples, a light to all nations, and glory to Thy people Israel." Hanna also, a prophetess, was present, and came up, giving thanks to God, and calling the Lady Mary blessed.

The History of Joseph the Carpenter

There was a man whose name was Joseph, sprung from a family of Bethlehem, a town of Judah, and the city of King David. This same man, being well furnished with wisdom and learning, was made a priest in the temple of the Lord. He was, besides, skilful in his trade, which was that of a carpenter; and after the manner of all men, he married a wife. Moreover, he begot for himself sons and daughters, four sons, namely, and two daughters. Now these are their names — Judas, Justus, James, and Simon. The names of the two daughters were Assia and Lydia. At length the wife of righteous Joseph, a woman intent on the divine glory in all her works, departed this life. But Joseph, that righteous man, my father after the flesh, and the spouse of my mother Mary, went away with his sons to his trade, practising the art of a carpenter.

Now when righteous Joseph became a widower, my mother Mary, blessed, holy, and pure, was already twelve years old. For her parents offered her in the temple when she was three years of age, and she remained in the temple of the Lord nine years. Then when the priests saw that the virgin, holy and God-fearing, was growing up, they spoke to each other, saying: Let us search out a man, righteous and pious, to whom Mary may be entrusted until the time of her marriage; lest, if she remain in the temple, it happen to her as is wont to happen to women, and lest on that account we sin, and God be angry with us.

Therefore they immediately sent out, and assembled twelve old men of the tribe of Judah. And they wrote down the names of the twelve tribes of Israel. And the lot fell upon the pious old man, righteous Joseph. Then the priests answered, and said to my blessed mother: Go with Joseph, and be with him till the time of your marriage. Righteous Joseph therefore received my mother, and led her away to his own house. And Mary found James the Less in his father's house, broken-hearted and sad on account of the loss of his mother, and she brought him up. Hence Mary was called the mother of James. (Luke 24:10) Thereafter Joseph left her at home, and went away to the shop where he wrought at his trade of a carpenter. And after the holy virgin had spent two years in his house her age was exactly fourteen years, including the time at which he received her.

The Gospel of Gamaliel

Gamaliel, known as Rabban Gamaliel, Gamaliel I, or Gamaliel the Elder, was a respected doctor of the law. He was the son of Rabbi Simeon and the grandson of the revered Hillel. From the Bible, we know that he taught Saul of Tarsus, later known as the Apostle Paul. Paul himself makes this declaration in his testimony to the Jews and advocated leniency toward Christians in Acts 5. Gamaliel's birth date is unknown, but he was at least 30 years of age when Christ was born. Gamaliel was already a prominent teacher of the law at the time of Christ's birth. It is even possible that he was a member of the Sanhedrin at the time. Several months after Jesus was born, wise men from the East arrived in Jerusalem seeking a newborn king of the Jews. The Roman Catholic Church teaches that these were kings, but they were most likely Chaldeans who studied the stars in the environs of Babylon, now Iraq. The arrival of the wise men in Jerusalem did not go unnoticed and their query about a newborn king caused no small stir in the king's palace. When the wise men told King Herod that they had seen "his" star in the East, the king took the news very seriously. There was no newborn baby in Herod's palace, so the king called in all the leading theologians for consultation. Gamaliel was certainly among their number, for he was too important to overlook. In the Mishna, Pesahim 88, he is called an "advisor to the king."

It was a well-known fact that the Messiah was to be of the lineage of David. According to the Talmud, Hillel was a descendant of the family of David. Some Jews even conjectured that Gamaliel could be the embodiment of that special personage and Gamaliel himself may have entertained the possibility of his son becoming the Savior of the nation Israel. Like Joseph and Mary, Gamaliel would have traveled to Bethlehem for the census recorded in Luke's gospel, chapter two. Hillel and Simeon would have been granted exceptions due to their age, for the Roman "head tax" was only for those between 14 and 65 years of age. Gamaliel, however, would have been expected to conform to the Emperor's decree. Might Gamaliel have occupied a place of honor in the inn where there was no room for Joseph and Mary? Perhaps his donkey had the honor of sharing a stall with the Messiah, breathing the aroma of fresh hay and straw while its master inhaled the stuffy air of a crowded inn! If Gamaliel did some quick calculating in the palace of King Herod, he would have realized, "I was in Bethlehem at that time!" Perhaps he concluded that an event of such magnitude and importance would not have bypassed a man of his importance. It is remarkable that unlearned shepherds experienced the visitation of angels and worshipped the newborn Christ in his manger bed, while highly esteemed theologians knew nothing of that pivotal occurrence in the history of mankind.

The Lament of the Virgin

In light of the enormous significance that the Virgin Mary would come to assume in later Christian piety, the rather leisurely pace with which the early Christians developed memories of her life is perhaps somewhat surprising. As is well known, the canonical gospels offer only very meager details of Mary's life, and despite the considerable narrative and theological importance of her infrequent appearances, these biographies of Jesus reveal frustratingly little about his mother. Paul, for his part, seems to know very little about the mother of the Lord, and other writers of the first and early second centuries seem similarly unconcerned with the events of her life. Although Justin would fust explore the theme of Mary as the New Eve around the middle of the second century, only with the near simultaneous appearance of the so-called Protevangelium of james do we find a significant break in the silence surrounding the life of Christ's mother. This early Christian apocryphon, it would seem, initiated the process of writing the Virgin's biography, beginning with the events of her childhood and her own miraculous conception. In the centuries that followed, other apocrypha would take up different moments from her life, including especially its dramatic conclusion, and collectively these narratives formed the basic building blocks for the medieval Lives of the Virgin. Beginning first with the seventh-century Life of the Virgin ascribed to Maximus the Confessor, Mary's medieval biographers sought to weave the strands of these earlier traditions into a comprehensive account of her life. This "Maximus" Life of the Virgin, in fact, established the basic pattern for many other Lives that would follow, and in transmitting the apocryphal traditions of the early church to the middle ages, it exercised considerable influence on subsequent Byzantine narratives of Mary's life. Whoever its author may have been, this late ancient biography of the Virgin, which survives only in Georgian, is a long-overlooked watershed in the history of Marian literature, and, as such, it deserves more considered study within the history of Marian literature.

Turning first, however, to the oldest Marian biography, the Protevangelium of James, one immediately encounters some remnants of an older generic confusion. Although modern scholarship has long classified this "proto-gospel" among the Infancy Gospels, as if it were primarily concerned with the story of the young boy Jesus, this designation is more than a little misleading. Originally titled the Birth of Mary, this apocryphon not only is not a "gospel," as has long been recognized, but also its primary subject is the conception and childhood of the Blessed Virgin, a point partially obscured by its rather odd placement alongside legends of the boy Jesus. Indeed, one wonders how this early biography of the Virgin came to be classified as an Infancy Gospel in the first place.

The Avenging of the Savior

The history of our Saviour's passion is about to display before us its bleeding mysteries and its awful vicarious scenes. The "Lamb of God, which taketh away the sin of the world" approaches the altar of burnt-offering. Bonds, the scourge, the crown of thorns, and the cross, present themselves to our view in the distance; and the "seven words" uttered by JESUS on the cross, sound in our ears, like the funeral knell of the kingdom of Satan, and like intimations of liberty and joy to the sinful race of man. O what wonders are we about to approach in our meditations! From the most appalling scene the world ever witnessed, a paradise of peace springs forth. From the most ignominious sufferings, we see the most glorious triumph emerge; and from the most dreadful of deaths, a divine and never-fading life arise! May devotion, humbleness of mind, and child-like faith accompany us in our meditations, and penitential tears become our eye-salve!

But do Thou, who hast the key of David, unlock for us the gates to the sanctuary of Thy sacred passion, and in the awful scenes of Thy sufferings, enable us to discover the mystery of our eternal redemption! Almost immediately after our blessed Lord had performed perhaps the most stupendous of His miracles, in raising Lazarus from the grave, after he had been dead four days, we are informed by the Evangelist that "the chief priests and the Pharisees took counsel together to put him to death." What a humbling view does this circumstance give us of the depravity of human nature as exemplified in these men, who, while obliged to confess the fact of the miracles which JESUS wrought, not only refused to accept Him as the Messiah, but even conspired together to rid themselves of Him by condemning Him to death! Neither will they be persuaded though one rose from the dead.

"Jesus therefore," we are told, "walked no more openly among the Jews, but went thence unto a country near to the wilderness, into a city called Ephraim, and there continued with his disciples." But "when the time was come that he should be received up, he steadfastly set his face to go to Jerusalem." With this object in view, the Lord takes His twelve disciples aside. He has matters of importance to disclose to them. Destined, as they were, to lay the foundations of His Church, they soon perceive His intention, and hang upon His lips with increasing eagerness. They probably reckon on some cheering intelligence, and expect to hear that the triumphant development of His kingdom is at hand. But what short-sightedness and simplicity do they display! O the mighty chasm which intervenes between their thoughts and God's thoughts! As though the restoration of fallen man were a thing of such easy accomplishment!

As if sin had caused only a transient disturbance in the relations between God and man, and occasioned a breach which could be healed, either by a voluntary declaration of mercy from on high, or by a confession of sin on the part of the fallen!

Acts of Peter

This is preserved separately in an early papyrus manuscript (fourth-fifth century) now at Berlin; the other contents of it are Gnostic writings which have not yet been published. I follow C. Schmidt's rendering of it. It has a title at the end: The Act of Peter On the first day of the week, that is, on the Lord's day, a multitude gathered together, and they brought unto Peter many sick that he might heal them. And one of the multitude adventured to say unto Peter: "Lo, Peter, in our presence thou hast made many blind to see and the deaf to hear and the lame to walk, and hast succoured the weak and given them strength: but wherefore hast thou not succoured thy daughter, the virgin, which grew up beautiful and hath believed in the name of God? For behold, her one side is wholly palsied, and she lieth there stretched out in the corner helpless. We see them that have been healed by thee: thine own daughter thou hast neglected."

But Peter smiled and said unto him: "My son, it is manifest unto God alone wherefore her body is not whole. Know then that God is not weak nor powerless to grant his gift unto my daughter: but that thy soul may be convinced, and they that are here present may the more believe, then he looked unto his daughter and said to her: Raise thyself up from thy place, without any helping thee save Jesus only, and walk whole before all these, and come unto me." And she arose and came to him; and the multitude rejoiced at that which was come to pass. Then said Peter unto them: "Behold, your heart is convinced that God is not without strength concerning all things that we ask of him." Then they rejoiced yet more and praised God. And Peter said to his daughter: "Go unto thy place, and lay thee down and be again in thine infirmity, for this is expedient for me and for thee." And the maiden went back and lay down in her place and was as beforetime: and the whole multitude wept, and entreated Peter to make her whole.

But Peter said unto them: "As the Lord liveth, this is expedient for her and for me. For on the day when she was born unto me I saw a vision, and the Lord said unto me: Peter, this day is a great temptation born unto thee, for this daughter will bring hurt unto many souls if her body continue whole. But I thought that the vision did mock me."

Now when the maiden was ten years old, a stumbling-block was prepared for many by reason of her. And an exceeding rich man, by name Ptolemaeus, when he had seen the maiden with her mother bathing, sent unto her to take her to wife; but her mother consented not. And he sent oft-times to her, and could not wait.

121

[Here a leaf is lost: the sense, however, is not hard to supply. Augustine speaks (quoting Apocryphal Acts) of a daughter of Peter struck with palsy at the prayer of her father.

Ptolemaeus, unable to win the maiden by fair means, comes and carries her off. Peter hears of it and prays God to protect her. His prayer is heard. She is struck with palsy on one side of her body. Then the text resumes.]

The servants of Ptolemaeus brought the maiden and laid her down before the door of the house and departed.

Acts of Paul

When Paul went up unto Iconium after he fled from Antioch, there journeyed with him Demas and Hermogenes the coppersmith, which were full of hypocrisy, and flattered Paul as though they loved him. But Paul, looking only unto the goodness of Christ, did them no evil, but loved them well, so that he assayed to make sweet unto them all the oracles of the Lord, and of the teaching and the interpretation (of the Gospel) and of the birth and resurrection of the Beloved, and related unto them word by word all the great works of Christ, how they were revealed unto him (how that Christ was born of Mary the virgin)

And when Paul entered into the house of Onesiphorus, there was great joy, and bowing of knees and breaking of bread, and the word of God concerning abstinence (or continence) and the resurrection; for Paul said:

"Blessed are the pure in heart, for they shall see God.

Blessed are they that keep the flesh chaste, for they shall become the temple of God.

Blessed are they that abstain (or the continent), for unto them shall God speak.

Blessed are they that have renounced this world, for they shall be well-pleasing unto God.

Blessed are they that possess their wives as though they had them not, for they shall inherit God.

Blessed are they that have the fear of God, for they shall become angels of God.

Blessed are they that tremble at the oracles of God, for they shall be comforted.

Blessed are they that receive the wisdom of Jesus Christ, for they shall be called sons of the Most High.

Blessed are they that have kept their baptism pure, for they shall rest with the Father and with the Son.

Blessed are they that have compassed the understanding of Jesus Christ, for they shall be in light.

Blessed are they that for love of God have departed from the fashion of this world, for they shall judge angels, and shall be blessed at the right hand of the Father.

Blessed are the merciful, for they shall obtain mercy and shall not see the bitter day of judgement.

Blessed are the bodies of the virgins, for they shall be well- pleasing unto God and shall not lose the reward of their continence (chastity), for the word of the Father shall be unto them a work of salvation in the day of his Son, and they shall have rest world Without end."

Acts of Andrew

After the Ascension the apostles dispersed to preach in various countries. Andrew began in the province of Achaia, but Matthew went to the city of Mermidona.

Andrew left Mermidona and came back to his own allotted district. Walking with his disciples he met a blind man who said: 'Andrew, apostle of Christ, I know you can restore my sight, but I do not wish for that: only bid those with you to give me enough money to clothe and feed myself decently.' Andrew said: 'This is the devil's voice, who will not allow the man to recover his sight.' He touched his eyes and healed him. Then, as be had but a vile rough garment, Andrew said: 'Take the filthy garment off him and clothe him afresh.' All were ready to strip themselves, and Andrew said: 'Let him have what will suffice him.' He returned home thankful.

Demetrius of Amasea had an Egyptian boy of whom he was very fond, who died of a fever. Demetrius hearing of Andrew's miracles, came, fell at his feet, and besought help. Andrew pitied him, came to the house, held a very long discourse, turned to the bier, raised the boy, and restored him to his master. All believed and were baptized.

A Christian lad named Sostratus came to Andrew privately and told him: 'My mother cherishes a guilty passion for me: I have repulsed her, and she has gone to the proconsul to throw the guilt on me. I would rather die than expose her.' The officers came to fetch the boy, and Andrew prayed and went with him. The mother accused him. The proconsul bade him defend himself. He was silent, and so continued, until the proconsul retired to take counsel. The mother began to weep. Andrew said: 'Unhappy woman, that dost not fear to cast thine own guilt on thy son.' She said to the proconsul: 'Ever since my son entertained his wicked wish he has been in constant company with this man.' The proconsul was enraged, ordered the lad to be sewn into the leather bag of parricides and drowned in the river, and Andrew to be imprisoned till his punishment should be devised. Andrew prayed, there was an earthquake, the proconsul fell from his seat, every one was prostrated, and the mother withered up and died. The proconsul fell at Andrew's feet praying for mercy. The earthquake and thunder ceased, and he healed those who had been hurt. The proconsul and his house were baptized.

Acts of John

The Acts of John describes several journeys of John, tales filled with dramatic and miraculous events, anecdotes and well-framed apostolic speeches Now John was hastening to Ephesus, moved thereto by a vision. Damonicus therefore, and Aristodemus his kinsman, and a certain very rich man Cleobius, and the wife of Marcellus, hardly prevailed to keep him for one day in Miletus, reposing themselves with him. And when very early in the morning they had set forth, and already about four miles of the journey were accomplished, a voice came from heaven in the hearing of all of us, saying: "John, thou art about to give glory to thy Lord in Ephesus, whereof thou shalt know, thou and all the brethren that are with thee, and certain of them that are there, which shall believe by thy means." John therefore pondered, rejoicing in himself, what it should be that should befall (meet) him at Ephesus, and said: "Lord, behold I go according to thy will: let that be done which thou desirest."

Now when all the multitude was come together to Lycomedes, he dismissed them on John's behalf, saying: "Tomorrow come ye to the theatre, as many as desire to see the power of God." And the multitude, on the morrow, while it was yet night, came to the theatre: so that the proconsul also heard of it and hasted and took his sent with all the people. And a certain praetor, Andromeus, who was the first of the Ephesians at that time, put it about that John had promised things impossible and incredible: But if, said he, he is able to do any such thing as I hear, let him come into the public theatre, when it is open, naked, and holding nothing in his hands, neither let him name that magical name which I have heard him utter.

John therefore, having heard this and being moved by these words, commanded the aged women to be brought into the theatre: and when they were all brought into the midst, some of them upon beds and others lying in a deep sleep, and all the city had run together, and a great silence was made, John opened his mouth and began to say:

"Ye men of Ephesus, learn first of all wherefore I am visiting in your city, or what is this great confidence which I have towards you, so that it may become manifest to this general assembly and to all of you (or, so that I manifest myself to). I have been sent, then, upon a mission which is not of man's ordering, and not upon any vain journey; neither am I a merchant that make bargains or exchanges; but Jesus Christ whom I preach, being compassionate and kind, desireth by my means to convert all of you who are held in unbelief and sold unto evil lusts, and to deliver you from error; and by his power will I confound even the unbelief of your praetor, by raising up them that lie before you, whom ye all behold, in what plight and in what sicknesses they are.

And to do this (to confound Andronicus) is not possible for me if they perish: therefore shall they be healed.

But this first I have desired to sow in your ears, even that ye should take care for your souls - on which account I am come unto you - and not expect that this time will be for ever, for it is but a moment, and not lay up treasures upon the earth where all things do fade. Neither think that when ye have gotten children ye can rest upon them, and try not for their sakes to defraud and overreach. Neither, ye poor, be vexed if ye have not wherewith to minister unto pleasures; for men of substance when they are diseased call you happy. Neither, ye rich, rejoice that ye have much money, for by possessing these things ye provide for yourselves grief that ye cannot be rid of when ye lose them; and besides, while it is with you, ye are afraid lest some one attack you on account of it."

Acts of Thomas

At that season all we the apostles were at Jerusalem, Simon which is called Peter and Andrew his brother, James the son of Zebedee and John his brother, Philip and Bartholomew, Thomas and Matthew the publican, James the son of Alphaeus and Simon the Canaanite, and Judas the brother of James: and we divided the regions of the world, that every one of us should go unto the region that fell to him and unto the nation whereunto the Lord sent him.

According to the lot, therefore, India fell unto Judas Thomas, which is also the twin: but he would not go, saying that by reason of the weakness of the flesh he could not travel, and 'I am an Hebrew man; how can I go amongst the Indians and preach the truth?' And as he thus reasoned and spake, the Saviour appeared unto him by night and saith to him: "Fear not, Thomas, go thou unto India and preach the word there, for my grace is with thee." But he would not obey, saying: "Whither thou wouldest send me, send me, but elsewhere, for unto the Indians I will not go."

And while he thus spake and thought, it chanced that there was there a certain merchant come from India whose name was Abbanes, sent from the King Gundaphorus [Gundaphorus is a historical personage who reigned over a part of India in the first century after Christ. His coins bear his name in Greek, as Hyndopheres], and having commandment from him to buy a carpenter and bring him unto him.

Now the Lord seeing him walking in the market-place at noon said unto him: "Wouldest thou buy a carpenter?" And he said to him: "Yea." And the Lord said to him: "I have a slave that is a carpenter and I desire to sell him." And so saying he showed him Thomas afar off, and agreed with him for three litrae of silver unstamped, and wrote a deed of sale, saying: "I, Jesus, the son of Joseph the carpenter, acknowledge that I have sold my slave, Judas by name, unto thee Abbanes, a merchant of Gundaphorus, king of the Indians." And when the deed was finished, the Saviour took Judas Thomas and led him away to Abbanes the merchant, and when Abbanes saw him he said unto him: "Is this thy master?" And the apostle said: "Yea, he is my Lord." And he said: "I have bought thee of him." And thy apostle held his peace.

And on the day following the apostle arose early, and having prayed and besought the Lord he said: "I will go whither thou wilt, Lord Jesus: thy will be done." And he departed unto Abbanes the merchant, taking with him nothing at all save only his price. For the Lord had given it unto him, saying: "Let thy price also be with thee, together with my grace, wheresoever thou goest."

Acts of Philip

When he came out of Galilee and raised the dead man.

When he was come out of Galilee, a widow was carrying out her only son to burial. Philip asked her about her grief: "I have spent in vain much money on the gods, Ares, Apollo, Hermes, Artemis, Zeus, Athena, the Sun and Moon, and I think they are asleep as far as I am concerned. And I consulted a diviner to no purpose." The apostle said: "Thou hast suffered nothing strange, mother, for thus doth the devil deceive men. Assuage thy grief and I will raise thy son in the name of Jesus."

She said: "It seems it were better for me not to marry, and to eat nothing but bread and water." Philip: "You are right. Chastity is especially dear to God."

She said: "I believe in Jesus whom thou preachest." He raised her son, who sat up and said: "Whence is this light? And how comes it that an angel came and opened the prison of judgement where I was shut up? Where I saw such torments as the tongue of man cannot describe." So all were baptized. And the youth followed the apostle.

When he went unto Greece of Athens When he entered into the city of Athens which is called Hellas, 300 philosophers gathered and said: "Let us go and see what his wisdom is", for they say of the wise men of Asia that their wisdom is great. For they supposed Philip to be a philosopher: he travelled only in a cloak and an undergarment. So they assembled and looked into their books, lest he should get the better of them.

Acts of Bartholomew

"Believe me, my brethren the holy apostles, I, Bartholomew beheld the Son of God on the chariot of the Cherubim. All the heavenly hosts were about him. He blessed the body of Mary.

She went and gave the message to the apostles, and Peter blessed her, and they rejoiced.

Jesus and the redeemed souls ascended into Heaven, and the Father crowned him. The glory of this scene Bartholomew could not describe. It is here that he enjoins his son Thaddaeus not to let this book fall into the hands of the impure."

Then follows a series of hymns sung in heaven, eight in all, which accompany the reception of Adam and the other holy souls into glory. Adam was eighty cubits high and Eve fifty. They were brought to the Father by Michael. Bartholomew had never seen anything to compare with the beauty and Glory of Adam, save that of Jesus. Adam was forgiven, and all the angels and saints rejoiced and saluted him, and departed each to their place.

Adam was set at the gate of life to greet all the righteous as they enter, and Eve was set over all the women who had done the will of God, to greet them as they come into the city of Christ.

"As for me, Bartholomew, I remained many days without food or drink, nourished by the glory of the vision."

The apostles thanked and blessed Bartholomew for what he had told them: he should be called the apostle of the mysteries of God. But he protested: I am the least of you all, a humble workman. Will not the people of the city say when they see me, 'Is not this Bartholomew the man of Italy, the gardener the dealer in vegetables? Is not this the man that dwelleth in the garden of Hierocrates the governor of our city? How has he attained this greatness?'

The next words introduce a new section

At the time when Jesus took us up into the Mount of Olives he spoke to us in an unknown tongue, which he revealed to us, saying: Anetharath (or Atharath Thaurath). The heavens were opened and we all went up into the seventh heaven (so the London MS.: in the Paris copy only Jesus went up, and the apostles gazed after him). He prayed the Father to bless us.

"All that is bound or loosed by him on earth shall be so in heaven; none who is not ordained by him shall be accepted." Each of the apostles was separately blessed (there are omissions of single names in one or other of the three texts). Andrew, James, John, Philip (the cross will precede him wherever he goes), Thomas, Bartholomew (he will be the depositary of the mysteries of the Son), Matthew (his shadow will heal the sick) James son of Alphaeus, Simon Zelotes, Judas of James, Thaddeus, Matthias who was rich and left all to follow Jesus).

"And now, my brethren the apostles, forgive me: I, Bartholomew, am not a man to be honoured."

The apostles kissed and blessed him. And then, with Mary, they offered the Eucharist.

The Father sent the Son down into Galilee to console the apostles and Mary: and he came and blessed them and showed them his wounds, and committed them to the care of Peter, and gave them their commission to preach. They kissed his side and sealed themselves with the blood that flowed thence. He went up to heaven.

Acts of Thaddeus

Thaddaeus, a Jew by birth, a Greek by temperament, and a scholar of Alexandria by circumstance and the Peace of Rome, to Marcus Ulpius Trajanus, conqueror of Dacia and Mesopotamia, to the Emperor Trajan, in Rome, greetings. Long life and good health most noble Caesar, and thanks to the gods you worship for keeping you and making you victorious in battle and bringing you safe to your throne as the worthy successor and heir of our late good and just Emperor Marcus Cocceius Nerva.

I write, great sir, as a man who has lived well beyond the four score years that, by reason of strength, are allotted to some men. It therefore comes as no surprise that the most able physicians of Alexandria, and therefore of the world, have assured me I am on my deathbed, and that I will soon be gathered to my fathers by virtue of maladies that, while perhaps not beyond the skills of Aesculapius, cannot be cured by mortal means. This assurance of imminent and certain death has provided a surprising sense of tranquility. I now fear neither the wrath of men nor the whims of gods. Neither have I the slightest concern for debates touching on any aspect of this world or on the hoped for world to come, in that I will soon vacate the former forever, and learn first hand what truths, if any, are to be learned in the latter. Socrates was surely right when he observed that death is either the most peaceful of all sleeps or the opportunity to meet souls who have gone before. Neither option should cause a dying man any concern, and neither concerns me. I can truly say that I am at peace, or, more correctly, I will be at peace when this testament to you is completed. Please forgive me the digressions permitted, and expected, from old men, be assured that my mind is sound and my memory good, and I will explain why my final hours are spent in writing the Emperor of the Romans, the oppressors of my people.

Acts of Timothy

The Acts of Timothy recounts Timothy's tenure as bishop of Ephesus. The Latin version of the text attributes its authorship to a certain presbyter named Polycrates. Timothy is said to have been born to a Greek father and a Jewish mother in Lystra. He was converted by Paul and traveled with him until he settled in Ephesus. After Paul's martyrdom under Nero, the apostle John, equated here with John of Patmos, arrives in Ephesus. Followers of the disciples bring to John various traditions about Jesus on loose sheets of paper, which he organizes into three gospels and assigns to them their traditional names.

Then he composes his own to fill in details missing in the other three. John is then exiled to the island of Patmos by Domitian. Timothy, who is still ruling as bishop, publicly attacks a local pagan festival called the Katagogia. In response, the revelers use their clubs and stones to kill Timothy. The local Christians take the bishop and bury him outside of the city in a place called Pion. Some Greek manuscripts add that his body was later removed to Constantinople. Under the reign of Nerva John returns from exile and becomes bishop in Ephesus until the reign of Trajan.

Catholic tradition states Timothy died in Ephesus when he was over 80 years old (1913 Catholic Encyclopedia). According to the first chapter of Foxe's Book of Martyrs, he died in 97 A.D. upholding the truth of the Bible. Foxe's states he was the bishop of Ephesus and was murdered when he told a crowd of pagans that their idolatrous celebrations were ridiculous.

Acts of Barnabas

Physician, I beheld and saw the ineffable and holy and unspotted mystery of the Christians, who hold the hope in holiness, and who have been sealed; and since I have zealously served Him, I have deemed it necessary to give account of the mysteries which I have heard and seen.

I John, accompanying the holy apostles Barnabas and Paul, being formerly a servant of Cyrillus the high priest of Jupiter, but now having received the gift of the Holy Spirit through Paul and Barnabas and Silas, who were worthy of the calling, and who baptized me in Iconium. After I was baptized, then, I saw a certain man standing clothed in white raiment; and he said to me: "Be of good courage, John, for assuredly your name shall be changed to Mark, and your glory shall be proclaimed in all the world. And the darkness in you has passed away from you, and there has been given to you understanding to know the mysteries of God."

And when I saw the vision, becoming greatly terrified, I went to the feet of Barnabas, and related to him the mysteries which I had seen and heard from that man. And the Apostle Paul was not by when I disclosed the mysteries. And Barnabas said to me: "Tell no one the miracle which you have seen. For by me also this night the Lord stood, saying, Be of good courage: for as you have given your life for my name to death and banishment from your nation, thus also shall you be made perfect. Moreover, as for the servant who is with you, take him also with yourself; for he has certain mysteries. Now then, my child, keep to yourself the things which you have seen and heard; for a time will come for you to reveal them."

And when it came to pass that they finished teaching in Antioch, on the first of the week they took counsel together to set out for the places of the East, and after that to go into Cyprus, and oversee all the churches in which they had spoken the word of God. And Barnabas entreated Paul to go first to Cyprus, and oversee his own in his village; and Lucius entreated him to take the oversight of his city Cyrene. And a vision was seen by Paul in sleep, that he should hasten to Jerusalem, because the brethren expected him there. But Barnabas urged that they should go to Cyprus, and pass the winter, and then that they should go to Jerusalem at the feast. Great contention, therefore, arose between them. (Acts 15:39) And Barnabas urged me also to accompany them, on account of my being their servant from the beginning, and on account of my having served them in all Cyprus until they came to Perga of Pamphylia; and I there had remained many days. But Paul cried out against Barnabas, saying: "It is impossible for him to go with us. "

And those who were with us there urged me also to accompany them, because there was a vow upon me to follow them to the end. So that Paul said to Barnabas: "If you will take John who also is surnamed Mark with you, go another road; for he shall not come with us." And Barnabas coming to himself, said: "The grace of God does not desert him who has once served the Gospel and journeyed with us. If, therefore, this be agreeable to you, Father Paul, I take him and go." And he said: "You go in the grace of Christ, and we in the power of the Spirit."

Acts of Matthew

About that time Matthew, the holy apostle and evangelist of Christ, was abiding in the mountain resting, and praying in his tunic and apostolic robes without sandals; and, behold, Jesus came to Matthew in the likeness of the infants who sing in paradise, and said to him: "Peace to you, Matthew!" And Matthew having gazed upon Him, and not known who He was, said: "Grace to you, and peace, O child highly favoured! And why have you come hither to me, having left those who sing in paradise, and the delights there? Because here the place is desert; and what sort of a table I shall lay for you, O child, I know not, because I have no bread nor oil in a jar. Moreover, even the winds are at rest, so as not to cast down from the trees to the ground anything for food; because, for the accomplishing of my fast of forty days, I, partaking only of the fruits falling by the movement of the winds, am glorifying my Jesus. Now, therefore, what shall I bring you, beautiful boy? There is not even water near, that I may wash your feet."

And the child said: "Why do you say, O Matthew? Understand and know that good discourse is better than a calf, and words of meekness better than every herb of the field, and a sweet saying as the perfume of love, and cheerfulness of countenance better than feeding, and a pleasant look is as the appearance of sweetness. Understand, Matthew, and know that I am paradise, that I am the comforter, I am the power of the powers above, I the strength of those that restrain themselves, I the crown of the virgins, I the self-control of the once married, I the boast of the widowed, I the defence of the infants, I the foundation of the Church, I the kingdom of the bishops, I the glory of the presbyters, I the praise of the deacons. Be a man, and be strong, Matthew, in, these words."

And after all these things had come to pass, Matthew the apostle of Christ appeared to the bishop Plato, and said to him: "Plato, servant of God, and our brother, be it known unto you, that after three years shall be your rest in the Lord, and exultation to ages of ages. And the king himself, whom after my own name I have called Matthew, shall receive the throne of your bishopric, and after him his son." And he, having said 'Peace to you and all the saints', went to heaven.

And after three years the bishop Plato rested in the Lord. And King Matthew succeeded him, having given up his kingdom willingly to another, whence there was given him grace against unclean demons, and he cured every affliction. And he advanced his son to be a presbyter, and made him second to himself.

And Saint Matthew finished his course in the country of the man-eaters, in the city of Myrna, on the sixteenth of the month of November, our Lord Jesus Christ reigning, to whom be glory and strength, now and ever, and to ages of ages. Amen.

Acts of the Martyrs

After the martyrdom of this blessed Stephen, suffered next James the holy apostle of Christ, and brother of John. Of which James mention is made in the Acts of the Apostles, the twelfth chapter; where is declared, how that not long after the stoning of Stephen, king Herod stretched forth his hand to take and afflict certain of the congregation; among whom James was one, whom he slew with the sword. Of this James Eusebius also inferreth mention, alleging Clement thus writing a memorable story of him. This James, (saith Clement,) when he was brought to the tribunal seat, he that brought him, (and was the cause of his trouble,) seeing him to be condemned, and that he should suffer death, as he went to the execution, he being moved therewith in heart and conscience, confessed himself also of his own accord to be a Christian. And so were they led forth together, where in the way he desired of James to forgive him that he had done. After that James had a little paused with himself upon the matter, turning to him, "Peace (saith he) be to thee, brother", and kissed him, and both were beheaded together, in the year of our Lord thirty and six. Dorotheus in his book named Synopsis testifieth, that Nicanor, one of the seven deacons, with two thousand others, which believed in Christ, suffered also the same day whereon Stephen did suffer. The said Dorotheus witnesseth also that Simon, another of the deacons, bishop afterward of Bostrum in Arabia, was there burned. Parmenas also, another of the deacons, suffered. Thomas preached to the Parthians, Medes, and Persians; also to the Germans, Hiraconies, Bactries, and Magies. He suffered in Calamina, a city of Judah, being slain with a dart. Simon Zelotes preached at Mauritania, and in the countries of Africa, and in Britain; he was likewise crucified. Judas, brother of James, called also Thaddeus and Lebbeus, preached to the Edessenes, and to all Mesopotamia: he was slain under Augarus, king of the Edessenes, in Berito. Simon called Cananeus, which was brother to Jude above mentioned, and to James the younger, which all were the sons of Mary Cleophas, and of Alpheus, was bishop of Jerusalem after James, and was crucified in a city of Egypt in the time of Trajanus the emperor, as Dorotheus recordeth, But Abdias writeth, that he with his brother Jude were both slain by a tumult of the people in Suanir, a city of Parsidis. Mark the evangelist, and first bishop of Alexandria, preached the gospel in Egypt, and there, drawn with ropes unto the fire, was burned, and afterward buried in a place called there Bucolus, under the reign of Trajanus the emperor. Bartholomeus is said also to preach to the Indians, and to have converted the Gospel of St. Matthew into their tongue, where he continued a great space doing many miracles. At last in Albania, a city of Greater Armenia, after divers persecutions, he was beaten down with staves, then crucified, and after being excoriate, he was at length beheaded.

Teaching of the Apostles

For the carrying on of His work, Christ did not choose the learning or eloquence of the Jewish Sanhedrin or the power of Rome. Passing by the self-righteous Jewish teachers, the Master Worker chose humble, unlearned men to proclaim the truths that were to move the world. These men He purposed to train and educate as the leaders of His church. They in turn were to educate others and send them out with the gospel message. That they might have success in their work they were to be given the power of the Holy Spirit. Not by human might or human wisdom was the gospel to be proclaimed, but by the power of God.

For three years and a half the disciples were under the instruction of the greatest Teacher the world has ever known. By personal contact and association, Christ trained them for His service. Day by day they walked and talked with Him, hearing His words of cheer to the weary and heavy-laden, and seeing the manifestation of His power in behalf of the sick and the afflicted. Sometimes He taught them, sitting among them on the mountainside; sometimes beside the sea or walking by the way, He revealed the mysteries of the kingdom of God. Wherever hearts were open to receive the divine message, He unfolded the truths of the way of salvation. He did not command the disciples to do this or that, but said, "Follow Me." On His journeys through country and cities, He took them with Him, that they might see how He taught the people. They traveled with Him from place to place. They shared His frugal fare, and like Him were sometimes hungry and often weary. On the crowded streets, by the lakeside, in the lonely desert, they were with Him. They saw Him in every phase of life.

Didascalia Apostolorum

Teaches all men in general abotit the simple and natural law, that what is hateful to thyself thou shouldest not do to thy neighbour. The Didascalia, or the Catholic Teaching of the Twelve Apostles and holy Disciples of our Saviour.

The planting of God, and the holy Vine of His Catholic Church, the chosen people who trust in the simplicity of the fear of the Lord, those who by their faith inherit the eternal kingdom, those who have received the power and communion of the Holy Ghost, with which they are armed and confirmed in His worship, those who have been partakers in the sprinkling of the pure and precious blood of the great God, Jesus the Christ ; those who have received boldness to call God the Almighty ' Father,' as heirs and partakers with His Son [and] His Beloved ; hear the Teaching of God, ye who hope for and expect His promises, according as it was written by order of our Saviour, and is in accordance with His glorious commandments. "Take care, ye sons of God, and do everything so as to obey God, and in all things be pleasing to the Lord our God." If any man run after iniquity, and oppose the will of God, he shall be counted by God as an heathen and an evildoer. Flee therefore and get far from all avarice and iniquity, that ye may covet nothing from any one, for it is written in the Law, "Thou shalt not covet anything from thy neighbour, neither his field nor his house nor his servant nor his maidservant nor his ox nor his ass nor any of his goods, for all these desires are of the Evil One. For he that coveteth his neighbour's wife or his servant or his maidservant is already a thief and an adulterer." He is guilty of abomination, like a Sodomite, from our Lord and Teacher Jesus the Christ, to whom be glory and honour for ever and ever, Amen. As also in the Gospel He reneweth and confirmeth and completeth the Ten Commandments of the Law. For it is written in .the Law, Thou shalt not commit adultery. But this I say unto you, as He who spoke in the Law of Moses, thus in person I myself say unto you, that every one who looketh at the wife of his friend to lust after her, hath already committed adultery with her in his heart. Thus he that lusteth is guilty as an adulterer. Also he that coveteth the ox or the ass of his neighbour is likely to steal it and to lead it away.

Apostolic Church Order

"Now this I say, that every one of you saith, I am of Paul; and I of Apollos; and I of Cephas; and I of Christ. Is Christ divided? Was Paul crucified for you, or were ye baptized in the name of Paul? . . . Therefore let no man glorify in men. For all things are yours; whether Paul, or Apollos, or Cephas, or the world, or life, or death, or things present, or things to come; all are yours; and ye are Christ's; and Christ is God's."

The church in Corinth had a most providential and even romantic inception. Sent by a special divine commission to Greece, the apostle had preached the Gospel in Philippi, Thessalonica, Berea and Athens amid much persecution, and finally arrived at Corinth, the great metropolis of commerce and culture. His work at first was greatly hindered by the opposition of the Jews, and he seems to have written to his friends in Thessalonica to pray for him that the Word of God might have free course and be glorified in this difficult field.

From the apostle's letter to this church we are able to form a very good idea of its condition. Living as they did in a city of extraordinary wealth and culture, they were remarkable for their intelligence and for the extent and variety of the gifts of the Spirit which they exemplified, but we do not find the same recognition or commendation of the graces of the Spirit. It seems probable that their intellectual culture was far in advance of their spiritual culture, and the result was a condition of sectarian strife and division which drew from the apostle the most earnest and affectionate admonitions and appeals, and which became at length the occasion for the most sublime picture of the supremacy of love which the Holy Scriptures contain. Let us notice at this time some interesting and instructive points connected with the membership and gifts of the Corinthian church, and more especially the unity of that church.

Apostolic Constitutions

That a bishop must be well instructed and experienced in the word. What ought to be the character of a bishop, and of the rest of the clergy. In what things a bishop is to be examined before he is ordained. That charitable distributions are not to be made to every widow, but that sometimes a woman who has a husband is to be preferred; and that no distributions are to be made to anyone who is given to gluttony, drunkenness, and idleness. That a bishop must be no accepter of persons in judgment; that he must be gentle in his conversation, and temperate in his diet. That a bishop must not be given to filthy lucre, nor be a surety, nor an advocate. What ought to be the character of the initiated. That a shepherd who is careless of his sheep incurreth penalty; and that a sheep who doth not obey the shepherd is punished. How the governed are to obey the bishops who are set over them.

That it is a dangerous thing to judge without hearing both sides, or to determine punishment against a person before he is convicted. That David, the Ninevites, Hezekiah, and his son Manasseh are eminent examples of repentance. Amon may be an example to such as sin with a high hand. That Christ Jesus our Lord came to save sinners by repentance. Of first-fruits and tithes; and after what manner the bishop is himself to partake of them, or to distribute them to others. According to what pattern and dignity every order of the clergy is appointed by God. That it is a horrible thing for a man to thrust himself into any sacerdotal office; as did Corah and his company, Saul, and Uzziah.

Canons of the Apostles

The first important part of the Old Testament put together as a whole was the Pentateuch, or rather, the five books of Moses and Joshua. This was preceded by smaller documents, which one or more redactors embodied in it. The earliest things committed to writing were probably the ten words proceeding from Moses himself, afterwards enlarged into the ten commandments which exist at present in two recensions. It is true that we have the oldest form of the decalogue from the Jehovist not the Elohist; but that is no valid objection against the antiquity of the nucleus out of which it arose. It is also probable that several legal and ceremonial enactments belong, if not to Moses himself, at least to his time; as also the Elohistic list of stations.

During the unsettled times of Joshua and the Judges there could have been comparatively little writing. The song of Deborah appeared, full of poetic force and fire. The period of the early kings was characterized not only by a remarkable development of the Hebrew people and their consolidation into a national state, but by fresh literary activity. Laws were written out for the guidance of priests and people; and the political organization of the rapidly growing nation was promoted by poetical productions in which spiritual life expressed its aspirations. Schools of prophets were instituted by Samuel, whose literary efforts tended to purify the worship. David was an accomplished poet, whose psalms are composed in lofty strains; and Solomon may have written a few odes.

The Epistle of Barnabas

After the salutation, the writer declares that he would communicate to his brethren something of that which he had himself received. "All hail, you sons and daughters, in the name of our Lord Jesus Christ, who loved us in peace. Seeing that the divine fruits of righteousness abound among you, I rejoice exceedingly and above measure in your happy and honoured spirits, because you have with such effect received the engrafted spiritual gift. Wherefore also I inwardly rejoice the more, hoping to be saved, because I truly perceive in you the Spirit poured forth from the rich Lord of love. Your greatly desired appearance has thus filled me with astonishment over you. I am therefore pursuaded of this, and fully convinced in my own mind, that since I began to speak among you I understand many things, because the Lord has accompanied me in the way of righteousness. I am also on this account bound by the strictest obligation to love you above my own soul, because great are the faith and loved welling in you, while you hope for the life which He has promised. Considering this, therefore, that if I should take the trouble to communicate to you some portion of what I have myself received, it will prove to me a sufficient reward that I minister to such spirits, I have hastened briefly to write unto you, in order that, along with your faith, you might have perfect knowledge. The doctrines of the Lord, then, are three: the hope of life, the beginning and the completion of it."

The Epistles of Jesus Christ and Abgarus King of Edessa

A copy of a letter written by King Abgarus to Jesus, and sent to him at Jerusalem by Ananias, his footman, inviting him to Edessa. Abgarus, king of Edessa, to Jesus the good Savior, who appears at Jerusalem, greeting. I have been informed concerning you and your cures, which are performed without the use of medicines and herbs. For it is reported that you cause the blind to see, the lame to walk, do both cleanse lepers and cast out unclean spirits and devils, and restore them to health who have been long diseased, and raise up the dead. All which when I heard, I was persuaded of one of these two: either you are God himself descended from heaven, who does these things, or the Son of God. On this account I have written to you earnestly to desire you would take the trouble of a journey here and cure a disease which I am suffering. For I hear the Jews ridicule you and intend to do you mischief. My city is indeed small, but neat, and large enough for us both.

The answer of Jesus by Ananias the footman to Abgarus the king, declining to visit Edessa. Abgarus, you are happy, forasmuch as you have believed on me, whom you have not seen. For it is written concerning me, that those who have seen me would not believe on me, but that they who have not seen might believe and live. As to that part of your letter that relates to my giving you a visit, I must inform you, that I must fulfill all the ends of my mission in this country, and after that be received up again to him who sent me. But after my ascension I will send one of my disciples, who will cure your disease and give life to you, and all that are with you.

The Epistle to the Laodiceans

Paul, an Apostle, not of men, neither by man, but by Jesus Christ, to the brethren which are at Laodicea. Grace be to you, and peace from God the Father and our Lord Jesus Christ. I thank Christ in every prayer of mine, that ye may continue and persevere in good works, looking for that which is promised in the day of judgment. Let not the vain speeches of any trouble you, who pervert the truth, that they may draw you aside from the truth of the Gospel which I have preached. And now may God grant, that my converts may attain to a perfect knowledge of the truth of the Gospel, be beneficent, and doing good works which accompany salvation.

And now my bonds, which I suffer in Christ, are manifest, in which I rejoice and am glad. For I know that this shall turn to my salvation for ever, which shall be through your prayer, and the supply of the Holy Spirit. And do all things without sin. And what is best, my beloved rejoice in the Lord Jesus Christ and avoid all filthy lucre. Let all your requests be made known to God, and be steady in the doctrine of Christ. And whatsoever things are sound and true, and of good report, and chaste, and just, and lovely, these things do. Those things which ye have heard, and received, think on these things, and peace shall be with you. All the saints salute you. The grace of our Lord Jesus Christ be with your spirit. Amen. Cause this Epistle to be read to the Colossians, and the Epistle of the Colossians to be read among you.

The Epistles of Paul the Apostle to Seneca

The earliest of the Latin fathers, Tertullian, writing about a century and a half after the death of Seneca, speaks of this philosopher as 'often our own'. Stoicism was in fact the earliest offspring of the union between the religious consciousness of the East and the intellectual culture of the West. The recognition of the claims of the individual soul, the sense of personal responsibility, the habit of judicial introspection, in short, the subjective view of ethics, were in no sense new, for they are known to have held sway over the mind of the chosen people from the earliest dawn of their history as a nation. But now for the first time they presented themselves at the doors of Western civilization and demanded admission. The occasion was eminently favorable. The conquests of Alexander, which rendered the fusion of the East and West for the first time possible, also evoked the moral need which they had thus supplied the means of satisfying. By the overthrow of the state the importance of the individual was enhanced. In the failure of political relations, men were thrown back on their inward resources and led to examine their moral wants and to educate their moral faculties.

The Book of the Covenant

The Bible was written for mankind, and thus everything it says is relevant to humanity. Man's chief purpose, however, is to glorify God and to enjoy Him. Fallen man glorifies himself and enjoys himself, or tries to do so. What does it mean to glorify someone? Basically, two things. First, it means to praise him. When a person brags about himself, he is glorifying himself verbally, with his words. When we sing the praises of God our Creator and Savior, we glorify Him verbally. Second, it means to do things to please him or to honor him. We spend most of our time trying to please ourselves and to honor ourselves. The Christian's labor, however, is to be accomplished for the pleasure and honor of God. When we glorify God, through life and lip, we find that we enjoy Him, and that we enjoy life. This is only natural, since God is the Author of life and the Creator of the world. When we do things His way, we cannot help but prosper in the long run.

God is a Person. He is interested in everything He has made. God is love, and He loves everything He has made. Thus, we are told in Matthew that God feeds the birds and that not one little bird dies but that the Father takes note of it. God even cares for the grass of the field. God has a personal interest in these things, and thus so should His image, man. This should teach us to treat God's world with care and respect, for we shall have to answer for it if we do not. In His law, God has protected the trees and the birds. If we take a man-centered approach to these laws, we might say that the purpose of this legislation is to ensure human prosperity. Such an approach to the law of God misses the most basic point.

The Book of the Rolls

Thou child of mortality, in whose body life and breath is, but in whose power it is not, why dost thou seek to evade the sufferings and distress, which the Lord thy God hath meted out for thee, that thou mayest be prepared to do his will, though thy mortal life should be sacrificed as the consequence, and thy blood should be required by the hands of persecutors, to seal the truth of the words which, by his Almighty Power, thy mortal hand hath been moved to write?

I say unto thee, fear not mortals, nor the face of mortal man, who is able to destroy the body only; but rather fear Him who is able to destroy both soul and body in hell. Bow down thine heart, O thou instrument in mortal clay, and suffer thy soul to drink in tribulation, as a thirsty ox drinketh in the crystal water. Have not all thy Heavenly Parents bestowed their strength, love and blessing upon thee, that thou mightest take thy life in thy hand, and put thy trust in God? Hast thou ever been forsaken by the spirit of God, when thou didst go forth, in obedience, to do his will? "Nay, nay, never, never, O holy Angel."

Then, make haste, get thee up from thy slumbers, thou child of sorrow, no more be faint hearted or dismayed, because of the word of thy God unto thee, that thou shouldst end thy days under excruciating sufferings; for none can find complete happiness, until they have suffered the final destruction of all the life that is natural and carnal. But rejoice in that God who hath called thee to suffer, that his word, pure and uncorrupted, may be brought forth to the children of men, according to his divine purpose: for to this end hath He called thee, and unless thou resignest to his will, thy soul will sink from his presence, and the blood of the unrighteous who would have hearkened to his word, had it been sent forth, he will require at thy hands. But if thou doest thy duty, and they hearken not, after they have had my word of warning placed before their eyes, or sounded in their ears, their blood must be upon their own heads.

The Clementine Homilies

Peter to James, the lord and bishop of the holy church under the Father of all, through Jesus Christ, wishes peace always.

Knowing, my brother, your eager desire after that which is for the advantage of us all, I beg and beseech you not to communicate to any one of the Gentiles the books of my preachings which I sent to you, nor to any one of our own tribe before trial; but if any one has been proved and found worthy, then to commit them to him, after the manner in which Moses delivered his books to the Seventy who succeeded to his chair. Wherefore also the fruit of that caution appears even till now.

For his countrymen keep the same rule of monarchy and polity everywhere, being unable in any way to think otherwise, or to be led out of the way of the much-indicating Scriptures. For, according to the rule delivered to them, they endeavor to correct the discordances of the Scriptures, if any one, haply not knowing the traditions, is confounded at the various utterances of the prophets.

Wherefore they charge no one to teach, unless he has first learned how the Scriptures must be used. And thus they have amongst them one God, one law, one hope.

The Recognitions of Clement

I Clement, who was born in the city of Rome, was from my earliest age a lover of chastity; while the bent of my mind held me bound as with chains of anxiety and sorrow. For a thought that was in me — whence originating, I cannot tell — constantly led me to think of my condition of mortality, and to discuss such questions as these: Whether there be for me any life after death, or whether I am to be wholly annihilated: whether I did not exist before I was born, and whether there shall be no remembrance of this life after death, and so the boundlessness of time shall consign all things to oblivion and silence; so that not only we shall cease to be, but there shall be no remembrance that we have ever been. This also revolved in my mind: when the world was made, or what was before it was made, or whether it has existed from eternity. For it seemed certain, that if it had been made, it must be doomed to dissolution; and if it be dissolved, what is to be afterwards?— unless, perhaps, all things shall be buried in oblivion and silence, or something shall be, which the mind of man cannot now conceive.

The Martyrdom of Clement

The earl of the sacrifices gave much money, and moved great treason and discord against St. Clement. Then Mamertin, provost of the city of Rome might not suffer this discord, but made St. Clement to be brought tofore him, and as he reproved and essayed to draw him to his law, Clement said to him: "I would well rather that thou wouldst come to reason. For if many dogs have barked against us and have bitten us, yet they may not take from us but that we be men reasonable, and they be hounds disreasonable." This dissension which is moved, it showeth that it hath no certainty ne truth. And then Mamertin wrote unto Trajan the emperor, of Clement, and he had answer that he should do sacrifice or to be exiled into the desert that was beyond the city over the sea. Then the provost said to him weeping: "Thy God whom thou worshippest purely, may he help thee." Then the provost delivered to him a ship and all things necessary to him, and many clerks and lay people followed him in exile. And the provost found in that isle more than two thousand people Christian, which had been long there condemned for to hew the marble in the rocks. And anon when they saw St. Clement they began to weep, and he comforted them and said: "Our Lord hath not sent me hither by my merits, but he hath made me partner of your crown." And three years after, Trajan the emperor, understanding this which was the year of our Lord one hundred and six, sent thither a duke, and when this duke saw that all they would gladly die for God's love, he left the multitude and took only Clement, and bound an anchor round his neck and threw him into the sea, and said: "Now they may not worship him for a god."

The Martyrdom of Ignatius

For Trajan, in the ninth year of his reign, being lifted up [with pride], after the victory he had gained over the Scythians and Dacians, and many other nations, and thinking that the religious body of the Christians were yet wanting to complete the subjugation of all things to himself, and [thereupon] threatening them with persecution unless they should agree to worship Demons, as did all other nations, thus compelled all who were living godly lives either to sacrifice [to idols] or die. Wherefore the noble soldier of Christ [Ignatius], being in fear for the Church of the Antiochians, was, in accordance with his own desire, brought before Trajan, who was at that time staying at Antioch, but was in haste [to set forth] against Armenia and the Parthians.

He then enjoined some to keep silence who, in their fervent zeal, were saying that they would appease the people, so that they should not demand the destruction of this just one. He being immediately aware of this through the Spirit, and having saluted them all, and begged of them to show a true affection towards him, and having dwelt on this point at greater length than in his Epistle, and having persuaded them not to envy him hastening to the Lord, he then, after he had, with all the brethren kneeling beside him, entreated the Son of God in behalf of the Churches, that a stop might be put to the persecution, and that mutual love might continue among the brethren, was led with all haste into the amphitheatre.

Then, being immediately thrown in, according to the command of Cæsar given some time ago, the public spectacles being just about to close (for it was then a solemn day, as they deemed it, being that which is called the thirteenth in the Roman tongue, on which the people were wont to assemble in more than ordinary numbers), he was thus cast to the wild beasts close beside the temple, that so by them the desire of the holy martyr Ignatius should be fulfilled, according to that which is written, "The desire of the righteous is acceptable to God," to the effect that he might not be troublesome to any of the brethren by the gathering of his remains, even as he had in his Epistle expressed a wish beforehand that so his end might be. For only the harder portions of his holy remains were left, which were conveyed to Antioch and wrapped in linen, as an inestimable treasure left to the holy Church by the grace which was in the martyr.

The Martyrdom of Polycarp

Polycarp was the bishop of Smyrna, today the city of Izmir, on the west coast of Turkey. He was part of the generation of church leaders who succeeded the apostles. According to one tradition, he was taught by the apostle John and was appointed to his office by the apostles themselves.

We owe the account of Polycarp's death to the Christians of Smyrna, who wrote it up as a letter and circulated it to all the churches. No wonder they wanted to tell the world: Polycarp's character and personal relationship with the Lord shine out in its simple words. The apparent defeat of his death becomes a triumphant witness to the resurrection.

Polycarp was martyred before the period of the great persecutions organized from Rome by emperors like Diocletian. His story reveals the tensions that were already building up throughout the empire, as Christians rejected the gods and goddesses that everyone else was worshipping. The pagans called the Christians "atheists" for this apparent lack of religious feeling. But as Polycarp made clear to a Roman government official, the real atheists are those who don't worship the one true God.

As the story opens in this adaptation of the Martyrdom of Polycarp, a local persecution of Christians has been going on. Some of Smyrna's Christians have already been put to death, and search parties have been looking for the bishop, who has been persuaded to do the prudent thing and leave town. Someone has just tipped off the pursuers that Polycarp is hiding out at a farmhouse in the country.

The Didache (Teaching of the Twelve Apostles)

There are two ways, one of life and one of death, and there is a great difference between the two ways. The way of life is this. First of all, you shall love the God who made you. Second, love your neighbor as yourself. And all things you would not want done to you, do not do to another person.

Now the teaching of these words is this: Bless those who curse you, and pray for your enemies, and fast for those who persecute you. For what credit is it to you, if you love those who love you? Do the people of the nations not do the same? But you should love those who hate you, and you will not have an enemy.

Abstain from the desires of the flesh and of the body. If anyone strikes you on your right cheek, turn the other cheek to him also, and you will be perfect. If anyone compels you to go one mile, go with him for two miles. If anyone takes away your coat, give him your shirt also. If anyone takes away what is yours, do not demand its return, for you cannot.

To anyone who asks something of you, give it to him, and do not ask for it back, for the Father desires that gifts be given to all from His own riches. Blessed is he who gives charitably according to the commandment, for he is blameless. Woe to him who receives. If a needy man receives charity, he is blameless, but anyone is not in need will be called to account for why he accepted it. And being imprisoned, he will be interrogated concerning his actions, and he will not be released until he has repaid every last penny.

Indeed, it has also been said: "Let your alms sweat in your hands, until you have discerned to whom you will give."

The Prayer of Manasseh

O Lord, Almighty God of our fathers, Abraham, Isaac, and Jacob, and of their righteous seed; who hast made heaven and earth, with all the ornament thereof; who hast bound the sea by the word of thy commandment; who hast shut up the deep, and sealed it by thy terrible and glorious name; whom all men fear, and tremble before thy power; for the majesty of thy glory cannot be borne, and thine angry threatening toward sinners is importable: but thy merciful promise is unmeasurable and unsearchable; for thou art the most high Lord, of great compassion, longsuffering, very merciful, and repentest of the evils of men.

Thou, O Lord, according to thy great goodness hast promised repentance and forgiveness to them that have sinned against thee: and of thine infinite mercies hast appointed repentance unto sinners, that they may be saved. Thou therefore, O Lord, that art the God of the just, hast not appointed repentance to the just, as to Abraham, and Isaac, and Jacob, which have not sinned against thee; but thou hast appointed repentance unto me that am a sinner: for I have sinned above the number of the sands of the sea.

My transgressions, O Lord, are multiplied: my transgressions are multiplied, and I am not worthy to behold and see the height of heaven for the multitude of mine iniquities. I am bowed down with many iron bands, that I cannot lift up mine head, neither have any release: for I have provoked thy wrath, and done evil before thee: I did not thy will, neither kept I thy commandments: I have set up abominations, and have multiplied offences.

Now therefore I bow the knee of mine heart, beseeching thee of grace. I have sinned, O Lord, I have sinned, and I acknowledge mine iniquities: wherefore, I humbly beseech thee, forgive me, O Lord, forgive me, and destroy me not with mine iniquites. Be not angry with me for ever, by reserving evil for me; neither condemn me to the lower parts of the earth. For thou art the God, even the God of them that repent; and in me thou wilt shew all thy goodness: for thou wilt save me, that am unworthy, according to thy great mercy.

Therefore I will praise thee for ever all the days of my life: for all the powers of the heavens do praise thee, and thine is the glory for ever and ever. Amen.

Made in the USA
Middletown, DE
12 May 2024

54229919R00088